$\mathcal{B}$

THE PREMATURE DEATH
OF PROTESTANTISM

FRED J. DENBEAUX

The
Premature
Death of
Protestantism

AN INVITATION
TO A
FUTURE

J. B. LIPPINCOTT COMPANY

PHILADELPHIA/NEW YORK

To Reinhold Niebuhr, a beloved teacher

Preface

Every movement is prey to its peculiar form of seduction. If Protestantism is to survive it must overcome its eternal temptation to express itself through polemics. A permanent polemic is self-destructive on two counts. On the one hand, polemicism is artificially sustained by deriving its energies from an inner uncertainty. It matters little whether that uncertainty is expressed by a ruthless intellectual apparatus calculated to bend the world to faith's will or whether the polemic is characterized by a relentless desire to reduce faith to what is congenial in the modern temper. Faith comes to a dead end both through the pretensions of theological imperialism and through the iconoclastic immaturity of a slippery apologetic.

Polemicism is self-defeating on another count. Its defensiveness prohibits faith from exercising grace and making a gift to the world. Harry Golden once said that Protestantism need not consume itself in self-inflicted shame. It had given the world universal education, the ballot and the writ of habeas corpus. Protestantism may yet give again, and when it does it will gladly undergird the creative vitalities of that civilization in which it participates. If it has the courage to trust itself it can make its contribution without first attracting attention by kicking over the gravestones of its ancestors.

I am debtor to many but shall express my gratitude to only one person. Margaret Clapp, formerly President of Wellesley College and now Principal of Lady Doak College in Madurai, India, encouraged these essays in more ways than one. It was she who taught me that theology need not be nihilistic and that creativity dare not set itself up as the enemy of form and taste.

FRED DENBEAUX
Wellesley College
May 1, 1967

[8]

Contents

THE PREMATURE DEATH
OF PROTESTANTISM

CHAPTER ONE

The Church
the World
and
Civilization

Protestantism must soon decide whether it will welcome or resist the crisis in which it flounders. On the negative side the community has revealed an enormous amount of vulgarity as various theologians have sought to communicate through popular media. By discarding all that secular man cannot accept, the church has given the impression of being all things to all men. By identifying itself with all that is easy, it has failed to stimulate life to the point where it is demanding. It is embarrassing to note that while the "Catholic" tradition has produced the disciplined poetry of Eliot, Lowell, Tate and Merton, Protestantism thinks to have fulfilled itself aesthetically by endorsing coffee-house art, folk singing and the guitar. And yet one may be grateful that Protestantism has been reduced to a minority status. Not only the fact that the Protestant has lost his prestige but, further, that the secular world views him with indifference if not contempt may soon make it possible for the believer to regain his innocence. If so, it will be because he is prepared to develop his faith as an art instead of hawking it in the market place.

It will not be long before the conventional[1] Christian discovers that the world at large cannot help but view him as a curiosity, and, like his Jewish cousins, he will discover that Christianity has a staying power which does not rely upon the approval of the civilization in which it participates.

It is unlikely that the Christian is going to solve the problem of his awkwardness by committing cultic suicide. By now he will know what the earlier disciples knew—that a Christian will always be a little out of step, a little alien to his civilization. He will also discover, if he has not already done so, that he will serve his civilization best not by obscuring what he believes but by being sure that his life, his thought and his piety reflect his lonely service to his art. As he composes his response to the mystery which shaped him he will forgo keeping a commercial eye on marketability.

Perhaps he will discover that a public-relations psychology diverts him from his task of living out of his faith according to its iron logic and not according to

[1] "Conventional" in this sense refers to the judgment that the world makes of him. In fact he may be one of the most unconventional of beings since, by finding his truth outside the current world, he chooses to define himself as a stranger.

[14]

those aspects which can be too cheaply grasped by the casual observer.

Perhaps he will discover what other minorities, painters, composers and poets have learned, that their demon is a truly jealous God and that they can serve their vision with clarity only if they forget the world at large.

Soon, the awful reality of God having been sacrificed by popularizing theologians, the church will discover that faith which is shaped for the eye of the casual observer is not quite the same as the faith which is practiced.

The death-of-God theology and every other attempt to jettison the eccentricities belonging to faith do not represent an honest description of inner life; rather, such definitions represent flirtatious responses designed to catch the eye of the modern man. Hopefully, Christianity may have entered into a more imaginative age, an age in which theological coquetry dies instead of the Deity.

And yet the Christian cannot be indifferent to his world even though he confesses daily that his citizenship is from heaven. Civilization, creative and important as it is, is not the mirror in which he finds his identity. At the same time he does not seek to erase civilization. What he seeks to do is to offer, out of his own peculiar resources, some word which may be helpful to that civilization in which he participates, but to which he does not owe an *ultimate* loyalty. If faith, refusing to identify church and culture, can yet speak a healing word, then the distinction between the logic of faith and the logic of the world is justified.

The Christian lives by the faith of the church, is

threatened by the world and enjoys the fruits of civilization. He is suspicious about the world because he knows that it has the power to deflect him from his faith. He is grateful for all the comforts and stimulations that a great civilization provides, but he is troubled about the relationship of his faith to the world of politics and art to which he has responsibilities and upon which, in a nonultimate sense, he depends.

The Protestant tradition assumes that the two worlds, church and civilization, must exist in two separate compartments. In part this view resulted from a reaction against medieval Catholicism's attempt to control both state and culture. In part it resulted from the Protestant's naïvely adopting the medieval psychology, unknown in the Bible, of an absolute distinction between holy and profane, sacred and secular. This rigid separation of the two worlds has created innumerable political advantages. The state as well as the arts are protected from piety, while individual faith flourishes free from official control. In America there is an added political factor, which many cherish as a blessing but which is at the same time a problem, namely, the explicit separation of church and state.

The rigid separation of the sacred and the secular has tended to create a cultural vacuum in American Protestantism. Judaism, on the other hand, has been much more fertile in setting the materials of faiths and imagination in creative tension. Thus one of the most impressive descriptions of Jewish faith comes not out of the synagogue but out of the novel.

When a Jew dies, who asks if he is a Jew? He is a Jew, we don't ask. There are many ways to be a Jew. So if somebody comes to me and says, "Rabbi, shall we call such a man Jewish who lived and worked among gentiles and sold them pig meat, trayfe, that we don't eat it, and not once in twenty years comes inside a synagogue, is such a man a Jew, Rabbi?" To him I will say, "Yes. Morris Bober was to me a true Jew because he lived in the Jewish experience, which he remembered, and with the Jewish heart."[2]

Protestantism, on the other hand, has created impressive political theologies (Reinhold Niebuhr's) but it has done little to stimulate the poetic imagination.

The contemporary literary renaissance in Judaism, represented by Saul Bellow, Bernard Malamud and others, has no counterpart within the Protestant experience. A theology which isolates faith from artistic creativity calls itself into question, and it has become increasingly necessary that Protestantism discover and explore its involvement within civilization.

At the present moment many religious thinkers are rejecting a faith which isolated the church from the world. The death-of-God theology, despite its somewhat grotesque and adolescent title, represents a serious attempt to close the gap between the church and civilization. We will do well to recognize its challenge.

The death-of-God theology, however, is only a very

[2] Bernard Malamud, *The Assistant* (New York: New American Library, Signet Book, 1964), p. 180. Judaism, of course, operates out of a different vision. Christianity depends upon the particularity of the church, both sacrament and preaching, in a way that Judaism does not.

[17]

radical form of a much larger theological movement of recent years. This movement, which for want of a better name we might call "secular theology," seeks to be attuned to the problems and realities of contemporary culture, with little regard for the traditions of the past. It is more concerned with life than with doctrine. Although it is a religious movement it often finds more affinity with secular thinkers than with theologians. Sartre, Camus and Beckett rank higher than Thomas Aquinas, Luther or Calvin. The movement is more stimulated by *Waiting for Godot* than by the Gospel of Luke. It sees the institutional church as a prisoner of its antique language. It takes "modern man," especially scientific man, very seriously. The "scientific" world-view, no miracles and no interference with normal processes of nature, becomes the key to what may be believed in the Bible. Since the God of the Bible seems to be "spatialized,"[3] and a Being who controls nature, and since that view appears to be contrary to contemporary experience, it considers much in the biblical view as mythological and expendable. What remains of the biblical view? Man and his hope—and Jesus, who is seen sometimes as the model of what man is at his best and sometimes

[3] It is easy to misunderstand the Bible at this point. John A. T. Robinson surely does when he says that "The Bible speaks of a God 'up there'" (*Honest to God* [Philadelphia: Westminster Press, 1963], p. 11). Actually the Bible views God historically and not cosmologically. God is always "back there" instead of "up there." He is not the God of the heavens but the God of Abraham, Isaac and Jacob, not the God who dwells in an upper story but the God of Sinai.

in a more profoundly symbolical way. The death-of-God theology is a daring attempt to secure cultural engagement but only by severing Christianity's relation to ties to its past.

The effort is interesting, but it is not without difficulties. In honoring the modern world it repudiates the past even to the point, if necessary, of ignoring the whole question of the existence of God. It suggests that faith cast its understanding within the language not of the Bible but of modern man. It finds an "at homeness" for its faith within the contemporary situation. By a special effort it thus overcomes the chasm, the artificial notion of sacred and profane, which in the past has often separated the church from the world.

But is the solution to a meaningless isolation of the church from the world to be found in a dangerous identification of the two?

While there is much to be said for a closer relationship between Christianity and civilization, a more basic point is the preservation of the church's freedom. One dramatic reason for preserving the church's separation from culture has a name—Adolf Hitler. In April, 1933, the "German" Christians published the following statement.

> A mighty national movement has captured and exalted our German nation. An all-embracing reorganization of the state is taking place within the awakened German people. We give our hearty assent to this turning point in history.[4]

4 Casalis, *Portrait of Karl Barth* (Garden City: Doubleday and Co., 1963), p. 52.

In their synthesis between civilization and faith, the German Christians went on to endorse the racial laws and to speak of the Jews as an "alien blood in our body politic."

Our present defenders of a *rapprochement* between culture and religion are not, of course, thinking in terms of a fascist state. Still, once the identification with culture is made, perhaps during the days of an affluent and liberal society, how will faith disengage itself if tyranny comes? In any event, should religion have become a department within culture in the first place?

Happily for the German honor a minority (26 per cent) dissented from the identification of the Christian faith with German culture. In the Barmen Declaration of 1934, the Confessional Christians declared that

> Jesus Christ, as he is attested for us in Holy Scriptures, is the one word of God which we have to hear and which we have to trust and obey in life and in death. We reject the false doctrine, as though the church could and would have to acknowledge as a source of its proclamation, apart from and besides this one Word of God, still other events, powers, figures and truths, as God's revelation.[5]

The death-of-God theologians, or their less extravagant colleagues, are welcome to experiment with a new relation between church and civilization. Others, such as the Unitarians, long ago tried to established direct relationship between faith and liberal culture. It is possible that many fruitful ideas will come out of the view which

[5] *Ibid.*, p. 56.

[20]

believes that "religion is the substance of culture and culture the form of religion," to borrow Tillich's words. Those, however, who have heard a voice which is not the voice of any civilization, a voice which refuses to become identical with man even at his best, must affirm in the style of the Confessing Church of Germany that the only *führer* is Jesus Christ and that he is the judge of every civilization and the captive of none.

Before we begin to suggest an alternative either to the identification of culture and faith or to their absolute separation, it will be useful to turn to the Bible, that strange symphony of voices which never quite says what men want it to say.

One must begin with a word of warning. Man does not find in the Bible something that he can handle, a set of definitions. The Bible does not have a fixed doctrine of the world. It does not even have a fixed doctrine of the church. The Bible has no frozen logic. Rather, it has a *voice*, a word which speaks to every man who hears while he tries to thread the needle of life. That word is personal, not abstract. The Bible is not a machine for grinding out principles. Sometimes the voice sings, sometimes it speaks and sometimes it is silent, but never does it produce a string of doctrines.

A doctrine is nothing more than a principle which can be applied without disturbing the center of one's being. A judge can apply a legal doctrine and not be personally involved. But when the Bible speaks the reader discovers that he is involved, that he cannot take refuge in doctrines. The voice heard in the Bible is the voice of God.

[21]

And when his voice is heard, when he sets his strange kingdom in man's midst, all human sovereignties collapse.

How then does the Bible speak about the church, the world and civilization? Are world and civilization the same? Does faith have the same relation to both?

The Bible begins with God's demand that man be a creator or "maker." Biblically speaking, creativity, civilization and "making" are synonymous, for each of them requires that man repeat what God has done, give shape to chaos. God gives man the power and the ineradicable responsibility to be a "maker," and by so doing makes him into a lord over nature. "Then God said, 'Let us make man in our image, after our likeness; and let them have dominion over the fish of the sea, and over the birds of the air, and over the cattle, and over all the earth . . .'" (Genesis 1:26). Dominion makes man become the creator of an order, a "maker" of civilization. Civilizations, the ordering of nature, exist because God wills that man shall be man and not animal.

Each man, the story continues, is called to be a "maker." One is called as a shepherd and another is called to be a farmer. This making is good and joyous. It is innocent. Abel's "making" is in the area of animal husbandry; Cain brings his creativity to bear on agriculture. Even though Cain murders his brother, he is not destroyed and goes on to become the father of cities. No condemnation is put on the original work of tilling the soil, nor of his later "making" of cities. Abel, whom he killed, was a shepherd, but shepherding is a civilization

[22]

as much as agriculture, and agriculture is as much a civilization as urban life except that cities may be more complex. Nevertheless the suggestion remains that the more advanced the civilization or "making," the more it is accompanied by pride, vanity and self-sufficience. Even if, as many scholars believe, the story of Cain and Abel reflects a tension between a later agricultural and an earlier nomadic way of life, such an interpretation only emphasizes the competitiveness and acquisitiveness which accompanies (but is not identical with) a more complicated civilization.

The voice goes on. Noah builds an ark, no mean feat, and organizes an escape from catastrophe. This specific "making" has been commanded. Man tills the soil and plants grapes, and for this work is not condemned. This is neutral "making." The first explicit condemnation of man at work has to do with the building of man's Tower of Babel. Men are confounded then not because they make towers but because they invest their "making" with pride.

It would seem, therefore, that in modern terminology one can distinguish between *civilization* and *the world* by indicating that civilization is innocent "making," whereas worldliness is the not-so-innocent use of "making" to turn man against God and toward himself. Thus Moses engaged in the "making" of a tabernacle, and that "making" was not wrong, but Aaron "made" a golden calf which turned man from God to something that he could control.

The prophets do not condemn the "making" of cities,

indeed Jerusalem becomes the symbol of the heavenly city. What is criticized is false "making," injustice. The prophets are not isolationists; they do not condemn even the "making" of a foreign policy, they merely condemn *reliance* upon it.

> Woe to those who go down to Egypt for help
>   and rely on horses,
> who trust in chariots because they are many
>   and in horsemen because they are very strong,
> but do not look to the Holy One of Israel
>   or consult the Lord!
>
> Isaiah 31:1

There is little difference, with one exception, between the Old and the New Testaments. Jesus accepts his own responsibility to be a "maker" and shapes rough words into memorable parables. Very simply he takes the trouble to use words well. He asks his followers to employ their capacity for all kinds of "making" in their service of the gospel (Matthew 4:18–22). Jesus does not criticize men for their civilizing activity; he merely warns them against placing their trust in their "making," or in the security they hope to gain from what is made. "Therefore I tell you, do not be anxious about life, what you shall eat or what you shall drink . . ." (Matthew 6:25). To the man who intended to "make" bigger barns and then take his ease, God said: "Fool! This night your soul is required of you; and the things you have prepared, whose will they be?" So, Jesus said, is any man "who lays up treasure for himself, and is not rich toward God" (Luke 12:20–21).

[24]

Caesar, or political life, has a just realm which is not to be confused with the realm of faith (Matt. 22:17–22). As one reads the Gospels, the impression grows that innocent "making" can become corrupt, and when it does it becomes worldly. Thus Jesus distinguishes his life and vision not from civilization which he accepts as man's obligation but from the world. He says, "They are not of the world, even as I am not of the world" (John 17:16). The disciples are asked to be vigilant lest their activities become corrupted and they serve the world. Again, civilization is not the world but it can easily become the world.

What the New Testament adds to the Old Testament is, of course, the person of Jesus, who introduces a point of decision, a crisis. It would seem that when innocence appears, it may invoke sourness in response. The activity of Jesus, his good works and his "making" pitches creativity to such a high level that those who cannot risk an investment in hope are affronted. Thus Luke

> Go and tell John what you have seen and heard: the blind receive their sight, the lame walk, lepers are cleansed, and the deaf hear, the dead are raised up, the poor have good news preached to them. And blessed is he who takes no offense in men (Luke 7:22–23).

Paul also saw Jesus in 1 Corinthians 1:20–25 not as the synthesis of culture and faith but as the crisis which forces a man either to believe in his civilization and thus become worldly, or to take the best that he can "make" and offer it to God, as Kierkegaard put it, with fear and trembling.

The transition from innocent "making" to worldliness can occur anywhere. The church, like everything else, is expected to be civilized. But just as the church must "make" its morality, its piety and its thinking, its art and its scholarship, so too can this "making" become worldly. When it chooses to believe in itself, in what it has made, it too becomes, whether it admits it or not, offended. All who are of the world are offended, whether in or out of the church, when they must choose between God's hope and their own proud despair.

The world, whether in or out of church, maintains its own kingdom. Wherever men, Christians or not, hold fast to their racism, their ruthless communism, their acquisitive capitalism, there the world, not innocent civilization, exists in its arrogance and defiance. Jesus and his kingdom threaten every convention, every act which undergirds the world's indifference and hostility to God's kingdom. If the church merely seeks to save itself instead of risking everything for his kingdom, then the church is merely the world masquerading as faith.

The Bible, then, evidently expects civilizations to be built, but often speaks in judgment on "the world." How shall one sum up the distinction? Civilization, as we have seen, is the peculiar act by which man expresses his God-required creativity. The "world," in an evil sense of the word, comes into being when men turn their "making" into an instrument to defy the sovereignty of the divine love. When men become "worldly" they

[26]

create a holding operation against God, an "ism." An "ism" is merely a new name for a Tower of Babel. It doesn't matter whether it is hedonism or communism, the belief in materialism or capitalism, the belief that man is primarily an acquisitive creature. It is not enjoying pleasure that makes hedonism a false god, but the *belief* in it (the belief in the pleasure itself and the belief in the "ism" that sanctifies it) which creates the idol. He who believes in an "ism" is so responsive to the lures of this world that he is tempted to place his faith in something other than the God of Abraham, Isaac and Jacob.

The foundation for a more creative relationship is found in the church's response to the biblical voice, its Trinitarian confession as found in its creeds. The Nicene Creed states:

> I believe in one God the Father Almighty, Maker of heaven and earth, And of all things visible and invisible:
>
> And in one Lord Jesus Christ, the only-begotten Son of God; Begotten of his Father before all worlds, God of God, Light of Light, Very God of very God; Begotten, not made; Being of one substance with the Father; By whom all things were made: Who for us men and for our salvation came down from heaven, And was incarnate by the Holy Ghost of the Virgin Mary, And was made man: And was crucified also for us under Pontius Pilate; He suffered and was buried: And the third day he rose again according to the Scriptures: And ascended into heaven. And sitteth on the right hand of the Father: And he shall come again, with glory, to judge both the quick and the dead; Whose kingdom shall have no end.

And I believe in the Holy Ghost, the Lord, and Giver of Life, Who proceedeth from the Father and the Son; Who with the Father and the Son together is worshipped and glorified; Who spake by the Prophets: And I believe one Catholic and Apostolic Church: I acknowledge one Baptism for the remission of sins: And I look for the Resurrection of the dead: And the Life of the world to come. Amen.

In the creed we are told that the Lord Jesus Christ is both the first "maker" with the Father ("by whom all things were made") and that he, "for our salvation came down from heaven." In Christ the dominion that God gave to men and the work of salvation that he accomplished are bound together. He is the Lord of civilization, the power which enables men to "make," and he is at the same time the power which saves men from the world and recreates in them the heavenly vision.

Many non-Christians have honored Jesus on other terms. They have viewed him as a great prophet and teacher. That is their right and the church must not diminish their way of looking at Jesus. Indeed, the church must learn from the creative insights provided by nonbelievers. Nevertheless the church looks at Jesus differently. It does not merely honor Jesus but sees him as the one who integrated man's understanding of himself and God: it is Jesus who binds the requirement of human creativity to God's will. Through the creedal union of God, Jesus and creativity ("by whom all things were made"), the church sees that its worship and service are an analogue to what is going on in governments, in concert halls and in museums. The church sees Jesus as the image which binds God's activity with man's. To see him as less would be to withdraw him from the complex of creativity and make him into either a cultic or a moral symbol.

At the same time the union of the Father, the Son and creativity saves the believer from thinking of God, as the author of Job seems to have done, as an awful impersonal force. All making, whether by God or man, is redeemed from being merely technical like that of a computer. Through the union all creativity, whether in the church, in the factory or in the arts, is invested with the quality of being personal and possessing human ends. The Christian understands God's "making" and man's to be bound not by the laws of machinery but to be invested with the personhood that one sees in Christ.

The Christ has to do therefore with both the "making" which we have been describing and the salvation which faith alone discerns. It makes no sense, therefore, to see faith as alienated from civilization. Nor does it make sense as the death-of-God theologians think, to *identify* Christ with culture. Why not? Because he who with his Father set in motion the process which *called* man to creativity is not to be found *within* human creativity. He is revealed only in his own Person, in the Word made flesh. But he who is revealed is also, with his heavenly Father, the one who placed on man the responsibility to be man, to shape, to make.

Christ is not to be found in culture. The Christian does not worship even Bach. The *St. Matthew Passion* does not reveal Christ. What it reveals is the calling that God and Christ placed on man. To be more specific, it

[29]

reveals what a great composer felt called upon to make as he reflected upon Christ's Passion, and considered what might be made through civilized music. The *St. Matthew Passion* is not God; it is man's response to God. Whenever one becomes engaged in the works of culture, whether economic or aesthetic or scholarly, one is not in the presence of God; he is in the presence of *human* creativity. It is a creativity that cannot be escaped if men are to be human, and a creativity which was made possible not only because God was in Christ reconciling the world unto himself, but because Christ was with God when God laid upon man the task of being creative.

The Christian position in regard to civilization is surely this. All that man is able to do and to achieve, all that differentiates him from the brute world, has been made possible because God in his peculiar way chose to cast his lot with humanity. History and civilization are the zone to which God comes. He who came to this zone is the source of all human creativity; and it is his coming, the unashamed bonding of God to man, which underlines the fact that man can and must distinguish himself from the nonhuman world.

The Christian does not take it for granted that man is man! His emergence, his creation, involved a special investment of imagination and commitment on God's part; man is not necessary to an ecological planet. A special being made in the image of God was gratuitously added: creative personality was inserted into the universe. Thus men are able to do more than collect acorns and build nests. They are given a special resource, one that does not come from what is ordinarily understood as nature, which enables them to shape rough justice, create poetry and make music.

It matters little whether man sees the process from the perspective of faith or not. He could not have become what he is if he had not been shaped for purposes eccentric to merely plant or animal existence. Insofar as God made man into a creative being his creativity cannot be annulled or even subordinated to either political or ecclesiastical piety. Christ is the protector of free creativity, the arts of civilization. The church, for instance, betrays its faith if, offended by the free activity of civilization, it seeks to deny what Christ came to ensure.

Civilization reveals the creativity that God has required from man. Christ reveals the creativity of God. The Christian thus witnesses to creativity both human and divine. He is sensitive and appreciative for all that man has made and he is a special witness to Him who has reconciled the world in Christ.

The church acknowledges that the Messiah has come both for those who, through the agency of the Holy Spirit, can recognize him and for those who cannot.

Because the creativity of man and the creativity of God are not the same, the church must not measure one by the other. The Christian must witness to Christ, but he must also participate in the creativity of man. He must not use his witness to Christ against the creativity of civilization.

[31]

The church has often been sinful because it has set the creativity of God against the creativity of man. The medieval church set itself up as a judge of what Galileo might think as a scientist and Protestantism set itself up as a judge to determine what a biologist, Darwin, might hypothesize.

The church has also been tempted to set itself up as a custodian of morals and has failed to encourage novelists to do their "making" according to their God-given imaginations. The church, if it lives by faith, has no business determining what can be written or what can be painted. Indeed, the church has a responsibility to encourage "making" even when the artistic imagination seems to threaten the frozen aesthetic values of the church. The church becomes worldly when it becomes insecure and fails to recognize its own boundaries. Too easily it identifies the gospel with convention rather than with creativity. Nowhere is this more apparent than in the sentimental paintings which decorate many Protestant churches or in the sad footnotes which Roman Catholic piety added to the magnificence of its Romanesque and Gothic architecture. Many visitors have been forced to blind themselves to the "bleeding-heart" school of painting which later generations placed on the walls of the cathedrals.

The church becomes "worldly" whenever it oversteps its boundaries, whenever it seeks to control and define what is not in its jurisdiction. There is nothing more worldly than a church which sets itself up as a police officer. More harm may have been done by ecclesiastical censorship, whether direct or indirect, than by the "immoralities" created by those who were censored.

The church must recognize that the creativity in statesmanship, music, and imaginative writing requires not only freedom from church control, but standards of criticism that piety, no matter how hard it tries, cannot create. The novels of Henry Miller, for instance, must be measured not by whether they are offensive to middle-class piety (they are) but by whether they fulfill the standards for a novel. What an artist writes or paints is in response to his humanity, the demand that God has laid upon him to be creative.

The church becomes "worldly" when it fails to be taught by the creativity of the world, whenever it retreats into a comfortable ecclesiasticism or whenever, as the death-of-God theologians do, it identifies cultural "makings" with the gospel.

If the church is offended because some civilized men do not appreciate the church, then it is also guilty of being worldly; it cannot ask faith of a civilization. It can only face the mystery of its calling by the humility of its witness. It cannot require or expect civilization to be the church. It must choose loneliness rather than ask civilization to forsake its freedom and become an arm of faith.

It is essential for the Christians to recognize that the church has a role independent of its place in civilization; it is not a branch of the government or merely an extension of any given culture. The church is always facing Jerusalem, not merely Washington or Moscow. Its witness is not to what men must and should do but to what God has wrought. At the same time it must not, by failing to recognize its boundaries, minimize creativity outside the church. It must not set itself up as a censor to the arts, it must not control governments. It has no authority to visualize itself in a superior position. Its witness is not better than the witness of the independent artist; it is not the sole source of integrity. To function, it must recognize that its role is radically different from that of civilization, but if it invests that difference with a higher prestige or virtue it obscures the Lord who called it to humility and not to pride.

The contemporary church is free from the temptation of a Christian cultural imperialism. It finds itself to be a minority. It dare not allow its reduced situation to tempt it to hunger for the fleshpots of Egypt, an earlier period when the church, whether Catholic or Protestant, virtually controlled its world. History has "humiliated" the Christian and, in faith, he can only be grateful that, like his Lord, he may occupy a state of lowliness. If he understands what has happened to him he will gladly acknowledge that non-Christians, like Christians, have a right to their existence. No man may be required to believe or may be diminished because he cannot.

Whether one is a Christian or not is no mere matter of choice. If a man is a Christian, even though his will has been involved, he knows that, in part, he is what he is because he cannot help himself and that he has been given a vision which he did not create for himself. The sensitivity and humility that belong to the Christian experience have been suggested by a young Catholic writer.

> I was born a Catholic, and many times that fact has prompted me to alternate between gratitude and despair: gratitude because I am quite sure that if I had not been born a Catholic I would scarcely have found my way into the Church. Like a certain French philosopher, I would have thought of it as "that dunghill." I have often felt despair because God came to me too easily, before I had a chance, entering my blood and bones through my mother's milk. It might have been easier to decide freely whether to believe or to disbelieve if I had been born an atheist. There are many things in the atheistic position that I envy, and struggle to make my own. But always there have been contrary experiences and reflections that made it impossible for me to become an atheist conscientiously.[6]

Civilizations are also not without their dangers. They too can become worldly, turn inward and avoid their calling to be creative. They may even become offended by the gospel and the fact that Christians witness to a vision other than that of the immediate civilization. So Hitler felt compelled to eliminate Jews and Christians. Their witness threatened a Germany which had turned from its humanistic task. It may be that there will be civilized men who will succumb to the world because they cannot accept the fact that for Christians the will of God is holier even than the national interest. No man is safe from the power of the world to corrupt.

[6] Michael Novak, *Belief and Unbelief* (New York: The Macmillan Co., 1965), p. 9.

[35]

But what shall be said about the future of American civilization? Prophets of doom can point to increasing chaos and criminality in the great urban areas. They note that large groups of young people seem to have repudiated the moral standards of their parents. Everywhere, it can be argued, there is drift and confusion. Community life seems to have lost its purpose.

But surrender to a psychology of doom, especially for the religious man, is surrender to the world. Perhaps the period through which we are passing, if we can find some shape for it, represents an opportunity for renewal rather than an occasion for decline. Our problem may be not that we have failed to hold on to our past but that we have held on to our past so firmly that we are unable to enter into our future.

As many civilizations have been destroyed because they clung too rigidly to their past, so other civilizations have leaped too rapidly into their future. Although much in our past is valuable, there is much that we must move away from if we are to become a healthy people.

The last century, as far as American history is concerned, does not represent one of the high points of human creativity. When we recollect our past we remember an age which conquered the frontier and made the first step in a change from an agricultural to an industrial society. By necessity it was an age of courage rather than beauty, of brawn rather than intelligence.

The age had the virtues that it needed, but they are not the virtues which help a people to acquire the art of civilized living. We are still so close to an age of violence, of prairies and cowboy heroes that we are in danger of forgetting that a civilization fulfills its obligation to "make" through its statesmanship, its music and its literature. We shall move forward and we shall survive only if we are able to create composers, painters, architects and philosophers who will help us to see a higher vision than the dramas of cowboys and Indians which still keep our imagination on the level of a child.

We are in an age of transition. We can go either forward or backward. We have created one of the most imaginative educational systems in the history of the world. More and more a college education becomes the order of the day, and we will soon have on our hands a citizenry which will be bored with the sentimental scraps left over from our past. An educated man needs a civilization which will keep pace with the development of his tastes. He will need a more significant exposure to art, to music and to literature if he is to go forward. He will need political leaders who will stimulate his mind in the process of collecting his vote.

But we may not be able to move forward. Going forward requires spiritual courage and it is easier to grow fat with the easy past than to struggle to enter a demanding future.

We may be so bound to the comforts of our precivilization that we have failed to recognize that God made man so that he might create ever anew. We fail to witness to the permanent solidity of God's coming in Christ when we become affrighted and pessimistic. When we would rather believe our fears than our faith, we have

[37]

surrendered to the world. Sometimes our witness grows weak and we whine with the poet:

> And how am I to face the odds
> of man's bedevilment and God's
> I, a stranger and afraid
> In a world I never made.

But we need not allow our fear of a more complicated civilization to cause us to lose heart. Once, long ago, there was a man who also had to face an unknown future. Because he was true to his witness he was able to gamble everything on the unknown. "Now the Lord said to Abram, 'Go from your country and your kindred and your father's house to the land that I will show you'" (Genesis 12:1).

Not in whining but in faith we walk forward into a future which will be more responsible, in which men will administer better governments, compose better music, paint better pictures. Putting away our worldly nostalgia for the past, refusing to hunger for the fleshpots of Egypt, we can act in faith and trust that the man, the humanity, that God has created will create better and more truly than ever before. Christ did not come that a civilization should go down the drain, but that man may, because God asks it of him, exercise a creative power which will cause the angels to cheer.

CHAPTER TWO

A Failure
of
Nerve

The Civil War in the United States ended a little over a hundred years ago. After the wounds had healed the nation gathered its energies and, within a few generations, changed itself from a semiagricultural nation to an industrial giant. Simultaneously during the century which followed this war it changed itself from a weak and uncertain power to a position of military supremacy. In the course of a century a divided and uncertain people had become one of the greatest powers in the history of the world.

Rejecting the rigidities of European politics and the dour cast of an imported Calvinistic theology, America prepared to march toward the light.

There were many prophets of the new hope. But it

was Walt Whitman who caught the spirit of the emerging age.

Of life immense in passion, pulse, and power
Cheerful, for freest action form'd under the laws divine,
The Modern Man I sing.[1]

And sing he did of the free man unencumbered by the chains of tradition.

I tramp a perpetual journey (come listen all!)
My signs are a rain-proof coat, good shoes, and a staff
  cut from the woods.
No friend of mine takes his ease in my chair,
I have no chair, no church, no philosophy,
I lead no man to a dinner-table, library, exchange,
But each man and woman of you I lead upon a knoll,
My left hand hooking you round the waist,
My right hand pointing to landscapes of continents and
  the public road.[2]

The twentieth century saw the fleshing out of the new optimism. Along with European socialism, America, in spite of its involvement with the profit motive, was able to provide both stature and security for workers, women, children and minorities. The New Deal, "progressive" education, the civil rights legislation of 1964—all coalesced to give substance to the new hope.

With the achievements of the new optimism few sane men can disagree. However, even in the midst of creativity a disenchantment set in. Something great had happened but also something demonic. The nation was un-

[1] Walt Whitman, "One's-Self I Sing," The Oxford Book of American Verse (1950), p. 275.
[2] Walt Whitman, "Song of Myself," The Oxford Book of American Verse, p. 346.

able to sustain its hope as it accelerated its power. It was only momentarily able to extricate itself from the darkness. A native American literature of both contradiction and disengagement produced a concern for the agony of inward existence rather than an extension of the dream. The very success of the effort had created an establishment psychology which meant that either, like Holden Caulfield, men were too sensitive to live in a "phony" world or too courageous to remain a part of it. In any case a literature exploring the "lower depths" emerged: a radical change was indicated. The age began with Walt Whitman singing of Life immense in passion, pulse and power and ended with Norman Mailer saying: ". . . all I know is that a man feels good when he commits a murder."[3]

The concerned observer cannot help but ask the question, What went wrong? Why did a dream collapse? It would be easy to say that the dream was pitched too high. Actually the dream perished because the philosophical soil on which it flourished could not sustain it and because the church was so busy attacking the secular dream that it failed to witness to its own vision. Let us discuss the latter first.

As one looks back upon the theological renewal in the thirties and forties the conclusion is inescapable that Protestant culture anchored its faith more in the Cross than in the Resurrection, that Good Friday was a more central holy day than Easter.

[3] Quoted by David Leitch in the *Sunday Times* (London), April 25, 1965, p. 21.

[41]

The most determined attack on the "innocence" of the American dream came from the Protestant theological tradition. It came from a movement influenced by the postwar European interest in the revival of Reformation theology. American religion, through the neo-orthodox movement was introduced to the "darkness" of Søren Kierkegaard, Friedrich Nietzsche, Fëdor Dostoevski. Initially influenced by the Swiss theologian Karl Barth, American theology, led by Reinhold Niebuhr, took a hard look at all doctrines of progress and all theories which did not recognize the limits of the human possibility. Niebuhr, especially, in his *Moral Man and Immoral Society* disclosed the powerful self-interest at the base of all communal and political life. Sin had been discovered and, indeed, had become fashionable. The impact of Niebuhr upon historical and political thinking assisted in the removal of naïveté and prepared the way for the *real-politik* which has since become increasingly characteristic of American foreign policy.

From radically different points of view, Reinhold Niebuhr and Norman Mailer came to a similar conclusion: Man is not basically moral and his hope is not to be fulfilled in any simple virtue.[4]

The attack upon man's sense of limitlessness may have been necessary but it effectively undermined his capacity for visualizing life in redemptive terms. Faith

[4] Reinhold Niebuhr is not, of course, a nihilist. He has created the most perceptive articulation of the classical Protestant mandate. That mandate always requires that Protestantism protect culture from idolatry. And to that end Niebuhr gave magnificent exposure to the illusions of liberalism.

[42]

became iconoclastic instead of proclaiming the good news. The neo-orthodox movement was dominated by the concept of the "abyss." Barth set the tone in his world-shaking *Epistle to the Romans:* "If I have a system, it is limited to a recognition of what Kierkegaard called the 'infinite qualitative distinction' between time and eternity. . . ."[5]

But, as William Hamilton has pointed out, neo-orthodox pessimism was generated by a depression and world-war psychology. Hamilton has recaptured some of the power of the Whitmanian dream in his essay, "The New Optimism—from Prufrock to Ringo." Rejecting the notion that grace can give a kind of stoic courage to face the worst, he argues that the conditions which created despair "can be overcome whether these conditions be poverty, discrimination or mental illness."[6]

The anchoring of the new optimism in the death-of-God theology was, as we shall see, abortive. Nevertheless, Hamilton rightly saw that the neo-orthodox movement merely corrected a superficial optimism; it did not spell out forever a jailhouse view of the human possibility. The neo-orthodox corrective of an optimism which did not do justice to man's capacity for evil soon made an alliance with a realism which failed to do justice to man's capacity to place limits on his evil. Every effort to freeze the biblical faith into a formula, whether optimistic or pessimistic, is doomed to failure because that

[5] Oxford University Press (London: 1933), p. 10.
[6] Hamilton and Altizer, *Radical Theology and the Death of God* (Indianapolis: Bobbs-Merrill Co., 1966), p. 169.

faith speaks both to the radical limits, the Tower of Babel story for instance, and to the radical new possibility, the good news of the gospel for instance. Jeremiah, whose name has often been a synonym for lugubrious pessimism, also looked forward with a vigorous hope.

Behold, the days are coming, says the Lord, when I will make a new covenant with the house of Israel and the house of Judah, not like the covenant which I made with their fathers when I took them by the hand to bring them out of the land of Egypt, my covenant which they broke, though I was their husband, says the Lord. But this is the covenant which I will make with the house of Israel after those days, says the Lord: I will put my law within them, and I will write it upon their hearts; and I will be their God, and they shall be my people (Jeremiah 31:31–33).

The New Testament, in part the product of an age of crisis and darkness, reflects both that darkness and a final triumph. The gospel leads men through the agony of judgment to the final benediction. The most optimistic statement, perhaps, in all literature occurs in the closing pages when the author of the Book of Revelation declares:

Then I saw a new heaven and a new earth; for the first heaven and the first earth had passed away, and the sea was no more. And I saw the holy city, new Jerusalem, coming down out of heaven from God, prepared as a bride adorned for her husband; and I heard a great voice from the throne saying, "Behold, the dwelling of God is with men. He will dwell with them, and they shall be his people, and God himself will be with them; he will wipe away every tear from their eyes, and death shall be no more, neither shall there be mourning nor crying nor pain any more, for the former things have passed away (Revelation 21:1–4).[7]

If Protestant theology failed, it failed not because it was critical of human pretension but because it did not develop a doctrine of grace which would enable man to recognize that he lived within a meaningful history.

Neo-orthodox theology, under the leadership of Reinhold Niebuhr, creatively illuminated the pretensions of socialism, pacifism and ultimately Marxism. Since Marxism was doctrinaire and possessed too high an estimate of human possibility it was no accident that neo-orthodox theology became more and more uncritical of those elements in our foreign policy which were too much an extension of the parallel idealism within the American dream.

While the State Department and Protestant theology could hardly endorse Mailer's insight, it is nevertheless true that, since Americans have become almost uniquely those who fight on foreign soil, one must conclude that Mailer's dark view of man has, in fact if not in theory, been shared by both the church and the government.

When a community, the church, has a faith and uses that faith largely to attack illicit hope, when a nation

[7] Christianity has often been tempted to interpret this prediction in the light of a Platonic eternity, but since the author had been schooled in the traditions of Hebraic concern for history, one can only assume that he meant what the words say, that God's renewal would provide new opportunities for human "making" rather than a renewal which would erase the human condition.

begins its modern journey with the conviction that the future is free and when both of them end in a virtual state of moral paralysis, one must ask the question again: What went wrong?

Surely one of the things that went wrong was that the church, substituting a corrective realism for romantic innocence, connived to create a psychology of despair.

The theological redefinition in the thirties was primarily concerned with the illusions within the American dream. As such it addressed itself to the task of "correcting" the world and man's "making" rather than witnessing to its own vision. But it was not only theological carping which corrupted man's courage to be but also his intellectual "making." His philosophization of his experience produced a range of ideas which gradually eroded his imagination and diminished his capacity for risk and creativity.

Modern man lost his nerve because a single and over-simple philosophical tool was made into the *sole* answer to life's order and its mystery.

Obviously, in a formal sense modern man is, by his own definition, a pluralist. How, then, can he be assured of making a single tool into the sole answer to life's demand and its mystery? Must one not recognize the powerful presence of upside-down Hegelians (Marxists), of existentialists and empiricists, of Freudians? But Freudianism was itself too limited in philosophic power to pose much of an alternative; and since existentialism was either ignored or treated with contempt, it was inevitable that empiricism would make common cause with an engineering and producing society. And when it did, it replaced the earlier Whitmanian romanticism with an aggressive pragmatism.

Through the triumph of empiricism, man ceased to be a thinker and became a measurer. Empiricism may be said to express the conviction that the content of consciousness came entirely from sense impressions and the "mind's" organization of those impressions into simple and complex ideas.

What empiricism did was to make *thingness* absolute. Thingness is what remains when external reality's connection with a universe of meaning is abandoned. In Platonism and the Bible, the two great philosophical theologies which preceded empiricism, there was no such object as an abandoned thing. Platonically speaking, an object was always connected with that which gave it its recognizable form. Biblically speaking, an object was always connected with the Author of all form. Both were summed up in the philosophy of St. Thomas Aquinas.

Although in all creatures there is some kind of likeness to God, in the rational creature alone do we find a likeness of *image*, as we have explained above; whereas in other creatures we find a likeness by way of a *trace*. Now the intellect or mind is that whereby the rational creature excels other creatures. Hence, this image of God is not found even in the rational creature except in the mind. In the other parts, however, which the rational creature may happen to possess, we find the likeness of a *trace*, as is the case in the other creatures to which, in reference to such parts, the rational creature can be likened. We may easily understand the reason for this if

[47]

we consider the ways in which a *trace* and an *image* represent anything. An image represents something according to a likeness in species, as we have said; while a *trace* represents something in the manner of an effect, which represents the cause in such a way as not to attain to the likeness of species. For the imprints which are left by the movements of animals are called *traces*; so also ashes are a trace of fire, and the desolation of the land a trace of a hostile army.[8]

It is the "trace" which leads mind beyond the chaos of sense experience and which enables mind to extract form and thereby achieve recognition. When objects lose, as they do in empiricism, their "trace," mind absorbs mere phenomena instead of a knowable universe. Thus Carl Becker says:

> Whirl is king, we must start with the mess of things as presented in experience. We start with the irreducible brute fact, and we must take it as we find it, since it is no longer permitted to coax or cajole it, hoping to fit it into some or other category of thought on the assumption that the pattern of the world is a logical one. Accepting the fact as given, we observe it, experiment with it, verify it, classify it, measure it if possible, and reason about it as little as may be.[9]

An abandoned thing becomes what Becker calls "brute fact." When things are abandoned they can only be observed, verified, classified and measured. And so empiricism rests on the assumption that man's relation to objects is fulfilled by the process of classifying them.

[8] *Summa Theologica*, Q. 93, art. 6.
[9] Becker, *The Heavenly City of the Eighteenth-Century Philosophers* (New Haven: Yale University Press, 1932), p. 16.

The problem is not the fact of the empirical method. It has richly enabled modern man to analyze and classify his experience. What has been dangerous about the saturation of our civilization with empiricism is that a *tool* has been made into a total philosophy. The decision to limit curiosity to the tasks of verification, measurement and classification has weakened the force of imagination. It is impossible to think poetically if one has as one's necessity merely the analysis of phenomena. The collection of evidence leads one on a path radically different from that of the pursuit of meaning.

The assumption, acknowledged or not, that experience consists of brute facts or abandoned things prohibits the asking of ultimate questions. The premodern man had a more open-ended curiosity. When Socrates affirmed that the unexamined life is not worth living, he did not restrict examination to mere classification. Socrates was a philosophical hunter seeking by his never-ending questions to find the spoor, the "trace" which would establish the relation of the naked fact to its purpose. Biblical man possessed a high capacity for synthetic judgment. Entering into a dialogue with his experience, as distinguished from merely organizing it, he was able to track the experience to what he believed to be its origin. The secular mind often assumes that biblical man, facing what he believed to be his God, exercised his piety by lying down and playing dead: the reverse is true. He wrestled with his God, often denied His justice and, in the process, produced an exciting literature of freedom and response. One has only to read the prophets, Psalms and Job to see that biblical man was not hypnotized by his confrontation but that through it he came alive.

Empiricism on the other hand, made dialogue impossible. Furthermore, the empirical psychology is oriented toward a simplistic view of experience. Not only is experience phenomenological and without ultimate meaning, but its randomness is grounded in sense impressions. When the ego ceased to be a self and became, rather, a wastebasket into which the "debris" of experience poured, man's reality became limited to his consciousness, or awareness, and the impact made upon that awareness by the world of sense. He could, to be sure, construct out of a multitude of impressions complex ideas, but since they were the products of consciousness they had no connection with the real world.

But curiously sense impression lacks involvement with the reality of the material world. Empiricism's concern is merely with the scar, the mark left upon consciousness, and not with the flesh in itself. The conclusion is inescapable that an unphilosophical Roman Catholic, attending Mass, is infinitely more involved with matter than the empiricist measuring the consistency of his impressions. The Mass leads outward to bread and wine and to God. Sense impressions lead back again only to consciousness and its principle of organization.

Only at his most minimal level is man a measurer. At his highest level he is confronted by constellations of experience which break all his yardsticks. He faces, as the existentialists have taught, a modality of contradiction between his hopes and his mortality. He faces, at least inasmuch as the literature of the past filters through to him, the anguish of the ideal. So thought T. E. Lawrence: "There is an ideal standard somewhere and only that matters and I cannot find it."[10]

But modern man restricts his curiosity to the surface organization of his experience. What he knows does not come from a confrontation with a constellation of meaning but with the "patterns" which his objective examination observes. Thus Thomas J. J. Altizer argues that a true definition of religion will be meaningless so long as thinkers remain "ignorant of the historical *phenomenon* of religion."[11]

And man the poet is externally frustrated because his saturation by the assumptions of empiricism forces him to ignore his ultimate questions.

By limiting curiosity and concern to the classifiable and measurable empiricism, he ignored those modalities which demanded dialogue instead of organization and description. Not only did man lose the capacity to talk about God, truth and beauty but, strangely for a secular age, he lost vocabulary to talk about *man* as well.

The triumph of the empirical psychology has played as much havoc with the humanist community as it has with the Christian. The traditional defenders of the humanist vision, Unitarianism, the Ethical Culture Society, the Friends, sound as defensive and as irrelevant as does traditional Christianity.

[10] Quoted by M. Chaning-Pearce, *The Terrible Crystal* (New York: Oxford University Press, 1941), p. 50.

[11] Altizer, *The Gospel of Christian Atheism* (Philadelphia: Westminster Press, 1956), p. 11 (italics added).

The nineteenth century, freeing itself from the ancient dogmas, substituted man for God. Neo-orthodoxy suspected, and rightly, that that was an act of idolatry. What it did not sense was that there was affinity as well as competition between the modalities of man and God. Neither are empirically measurable and each modality can be grasped only by the imagination. But empiricism can view the imagination as only self-indulgent subjectivity.

Is humanism passé in the modern world? Carl Becker, a vigorous interpreter of history from empirical presuppositions, says:

> What is peculiar to the modern mind is the disposition and determination to regard ideas and concepts, the truth of things as well as the things themselves, as changing entities, the character and significance of which at any given time can be fully grasped only by regarding them as points in an endless process of differentiation, of unfolding, of waste and repair.[12]

When experience is reduced, as it must be in empiricism, to an "endless process," all universals collapse. Man goes down the drain when thought is restricted to the tedious system of classifying man and his cultures as mere phenomena.

Not only is it impossible to think empirically about so universal a being as man, but it is also impossible, since only the immediate can be measured, to think creatively about the past.

Human experience, however, is not limited to the

[12] Becker, *op. cit.*, p. 19.

chaos of the immediate. Man's experiences, when he is not fettered by a compulsive philosophy, arise out of islands of meaning (modalities) within the endless rush of experience. He experiences persons and events each of which constitutes a constellation of meaning which cannot be reduced to sense experience or to mere reflection upon it. Modalities such as the names of Shakespeare, Schweitzer and Lincoln are more than phenomena: they are modalities which have the power to evoke genuine dialogue. Indeed, the greatest illusion of our time is that sense impressions are the primary reality. They are, in fact, a myth, a reductionist myth, but a wanton fantasy nevertheless. William Blake, in *Jerusalem*, revealed the meaninglessness of reducing experience to mere fact when he said:

For a Tear is an Intellectual thing.

The triumph of empiricism has been as subtle as it is pervasive. There was a time, prior to the erosion of unity in the communist world, when anticommunists viewed international communism as a monolithic structure. There was also a time, prior to good Pope John, when many Protestants looked upon the Roman Church as possessing a seamless structure. Yet both Roman Catholicism and communism seem almost disorganized when compared to the establishment of the empirical method. It and it alone has achieved the quality of self-evidency. It has become the dogma of the twentieth century.

Nowhere has this unconscious intrigue against pluralism been more successful than in its influence over contemporary theology. Whereas earlier thinkers like Reinhold Niebuhr still appealed to the pre-empirical modalities of sin and redemption, the contemporary theologian must, if he is to be heard in the world, surrender his interest in the past and accept the limits imposed by a secular understanding.

In this sense the present form of secularism differs from earlier attempts to find truth outside the ecclesiastical institution. For secularism today means a society which is congenial only to the time zone that empiricism will tolerate, the immediate and the contemporary. A Nietzsche would be as uncomfortable within the prison-house of modern thinking as are those Christians who are trying to comprehend the relation of their legacy to a world that cannot even imagine the past.

Insofar as contemporary theology identifies itself with secularism, it also declares the past and its claims to be off bounds to honest dialogue. Altizer reflects the new emancipation:

> Every American can in some sense join James Baldwin in saying that the Chartres Cathedral is not a part of his past. As Americans, our past is simply an extension of a horizontal present, and apart from a few rapidly vanishing insular regions of the nation, the contemporary American cannot associate a living moment with a moment of the past.[13]

While not all contemporary theologians would put the matters so radically, many would reflect both the notion

[13] Altizer and Hamilton, *Radical Theology and the Death of God*, p. 9.

[54]

that truth and the form of its proclamation is culturally conditioned and a rather anxious desire to appeal to the world-view of the modern man. While both of these concerns have some validity, when they are stated in a radical form they merely surrender to the simplistic thinking of the empirical world-view.

The assumption that the forms of the past must be radically criticized is, of course, shared by every scholar. But those not handcuffed by empiricism and the authority of the modern mood consider the possibility that the past has produced some concrete wisdom which is not absolutely time-conditioned. Athanasius, the defender of the Nicene Creed, was able, according to C. N. Cochrane, to give radical redefinition to the nature of human experience without erasing the wisdom which had preceded the Christian understanding.

> Athanasius was, indeed, a man of one idea, but that idea was of profound and far-reaching consequence. To him it was evident that, if Graeco-Roman speculation had issued in insoluble puzzles, this was the inevitable result of its having accepted a vicious or defective starting point. And, in Trinitarianism, he found a basic principle broad and inclusive enough to bear the weight of the conclusions derived from it and to sustain, rather than stifle, the life of religion and philosophy. In this connection it should be noticed that, in referring to the Trinity, the term he regularly employs is *arché* (ἀρχή), a word consecrated by immemorial usage among the Greeks; and by adopting it, Athanasius associates himself with the spirit of Greek thought from its beginnings with Thales and the naturalists. But in the character which he ascribes to or rather discovers in it, Athanasius

[55]

departs radically from the Greek philosophic tradition. For while the Greeks sought for this *arché* in "nature," Athanasius perceived that it was not to be found either "within" or "without" the frontiers of the physical world. And, while they conceived of it as a "cause" or rather as the "cause of causes," he contended that what is supposed in the nexus of events within the order of time and space could not be casually related to them. Knowledge of such a principle, therefore, differed *toto caelo* from knowledge of nature; and it was not to be attained by pursuing the chain of natural causation to its limit. In other words it was a matter of direct and immediate apprehension to be recognized by "its working and power." As such, the consciousness of it was part of the original spiritual legacy of mankind.[14]

By placing his radical insights within the context of "The original spiritual legacy of mankind," Athanasius saved himself from becoming merely the prisoner of his own century. Indeed, a willingness to take the past seriously has distinguished Christian theology in its creative periods. There were, to be sure, churchmen who erased the modalities of the past. Tertullian, whose stance is an analogue to that of Altizer's, held that there could be no concord between Athens and Jerusalem. Yet the church constantly resisted the efforts of those who sought to separate what the church was trying to do from the spiritual legacy of mankind.

If the European vision, the legacy from Socrates through Chartres, was the bearer of a creative vision it was such because the great classical theologians recognized

[14] Cochrane, *Christianity and Classical Culture* (New York: Oxford University Press, Galaxy Book, 1956), pp. 361–362.

[56]

that man was more than the recipient of, in Becker's words, "an endless process of differentiation," that he was indeed defined by his continuing legacy.

Medievalism, whatever its eccentricities, whatever its numerous temptations to withdraw into an empty mysticism, honored that ancient legacy to which it gave new form.

St. Thomas' conviction that true knowledge began not with the "inner life" but with the physical cosmos and the movement via the principle of causality to God was an analogue to the doctrine of transubstantiation where wine and bread became the instruments through which the living God was perceived. The glorification of the sensual world would not have been possible had the final inheritance of the earlier spiritualism, radical asceticism, triumphed. The marriage of sense and purpose is illustrated by the Abbot Suger, who placed the following poem on the central west portal doors of his beloved St.-Denis.

> Whoever thou art, if thou seekest
> to extol the glory of these doors,
>
> Marvel not at the gold and expense but at
> the craftsmanship of the work
>
> Bright is the noble work; but, being
> nobly bright, the work
>
> Should brighten the minds so that
> they may travel, through the true lights,
>
> To the True Light where Christ is
> the true door.

> In what manner it be inherent in
>   this world the golden door defines:
>
> The dull mind rises to truth
>   through that which is material
>
> And in seeing this light, is resurrected
>   from its former submersion.[15]

Thus the medieval vision and empiricism part company at the question of the sobriety and the integrity of sense impression. Whereas for Professor Becker sense provides merely an endless (and metaphysically empty) process, for Suger "the dull mind rises to truth through that which is material."

Contemporary theology is not so fortunate, for with the triumph of secularism the possibility of a legacy disappeared. And when the immediate and the contemporary became enthroned, then the past could only become *"an extension of the horizontal present"* (Altizer). Time, as it is ordinarily understood, disappeared.

With the triumph of contemporaneity there is a great danger that theology may become so isolated from the past that the church may literally become an illiterate community. William Hamilton illustrates the isolation of the religiously oriented thinker from the legacy of the past.

> What does the theologian read? Does he read religious books in hardcovers? Less and less, perhaps not at all, except when he has a free copy for review or a bibliography to prepare. He has been unable to read books of

[15] Erwin Panofsky, *Abbot Suger* (Princeton: Princeton University Press, 1946), p. 23.

sermons for a long time, and he has recently found that he practically never reads a book of theology for the sheer fun of it. He reads a lot of paperbacks, articles and reviews. Just as less and less theological writing is being put into books, the theological reader is reading fewer and fewer books.[16]

So much for the original spiritual legacy of mankind.

Does not the severance of man from his past represent a kind of retreat? Just as the monk left the complex world and entered into a controlled environment does not the contemporary theologian, by concerning himself only with the contemporary, enter a world which he can manage?

Altizer is convinced that Christianity has betrayed Jesus and that ". . . we cannot truly pronounce the name of Jesus if we isolate his name from the contingency and the actuality of our concrete existence in the world."[17] He does not, apparently, include within his conception of concrete existence the dialogue between legacy (since the church betrayed Jesus) and contemporaneity. Thus, speaking of Jesus, he says: ". . . the historical reality and power of his name as concealing a hidden but universal process of redemption and transformation, a process that has only been known in a reversed or religious form to his ecclesiastical followers."[18]

The notion that the universal process of redemption has been known in only a *reversed* form by the followers

---

[16] Altizer and Hamilton, *Radical Theology and the Death of God*, p. 89.
[17] Altizer, *The Gospel of Christian Atheism*, pp. 56–57.
[18] *Ibid.*, p. 56.

of Jesus effectively denies not simply the concept of legacy but also the possibility of an incarnation. If the cult or community of disciples is doomed to misunderstand, then Jesus is not connected with the real world. For the concept of the religious community effectively communicating its legacy is as real as the concept of the political community communicating its inheritance. One might as well argue that the democratic ideal has been understood in only a reversed form by its adherents. The assumption that the cult can understand, can have an honest and a communicable legacy, is an audacious way of affirming that God is involved in the real world, the world of legacy, of discipleship.

But Altizer is not alone in his suspicion of full meaning of temporality. The elimination of the past means the erasure of all form whether liturgical or intellectual. Thus, for William Hamilton, "the theologian is alienated from the Bible, just as he is alienated from God and the church."[19]

Indeed the institutional (thus visible and discussable) church is not necessary. Like Altizer, Hamilton appeals to the universal, wherever "Christ is being formed among men in the world." Hamilton recognizes the lack of concreteness in his view when he goes on to say: "This is a very vague way of describing his feelings about the community, even though it has no outlines, no preaching, sacraments or liturgy."[20]

[19] Altizer and Hamilton, Radical Theology and the Death of God, p. 90.
[20] Ibid., p. 91.

One detects within the arguments of the defenders of a situational ethic a similar inability to take the past seriously. Just as the ultimate cannot reside within the empirical particularity of an institution, so too the ultimate cannot be contained within human wisdom, morality or principles. Thus Joseph Fletcher argues: "When love reigns, not law, the decisions of conscience are relative."[21] And from this premise he deduces that, under certain circumstances, what traditional morality would call murder or adultery can constitute an act of love. In each case it is the past, whether the church, the Bible or morality, which is considered to be suspect. In each case man abandons the past, lives freely in the world and meets love and Christ. Whether this is possible or desirable is not the argument. What is interesting is that in each case the possibility that God has committed himself in a *recognizable* form has been abandoned. And with the abandonment of the form we face the loss of knowledge and respect for the integrity of the knowing process.

It should be clear that the use of the word "legacy" is an alternative to the word "institutional" as well as a criticism of the formlessness of contemporary thinking. A legacy can be multiple and need not be frozen into a doctrine. Thus, as we enter the ecumenical age, the age of true dialogue, it is becoming clear that many will find that their legacy is, to choose a few points of concretion, Catholic, Protestant, Jewish and "Platonic."

[21] Fletcher, *Situation Ethics* (Philadelphia: Westminster Press, 1966), p. 143.

Legacy enables one to escape the present contempt for institutional religion without being a slave to the institution. Christianity, by nature, is synthetic, opening itself as it does to the Hebraic and to the Classical. It is thus possible to think of legacy both in terms of open confessionalism and in relation to those who, troubled by the shapelessness of sheer contemporaneity, seek to absorb something from the vitalities of the past. It may even be possible that the time will come when a concept of legacy will be freed from a confessional requirement so that that past can be shaped by those who are bound by the Christian synthesis and by those who will see themselves as friends and critics of that synthesis.

A theology incapable of joining past and present, unwilling to recognize that form is more than distortion, can only move toward shapelessness. An ethic which is purely contextual and a view of Jesus unrelated to a legacy cannot speak of man any more than it can speak of God. It can only discuss fragments.

Modern man seems to have lost his nerve. It is Nonno in *The Night of the Iguana* who most poignantly reflects his surrender to formless universalism.

> Sometimes while night obscures the tree
> The zenith of its life will be
> Gone past forever, and from thence
> A second history will commence.
>
> A chronicle no longer gold,
> A bargaining with mist and mould,
> And finally the broken stem
> The plummeting to earth; and then

An intercourse not well designed
For beings of a golden kind
Whose native green must arch above
The earth's obscene, corrupting love.[22]

When man begins to believe that all that the earth offers is its "obscene, corrupting love," then he must discover that he has come full circle, that Whitman's rejection of tradition ends in a despair similar to that of tradition when it becomes doctrinaire. Precisely at this point Christianity must speak. To youth with its suspicion that corporate existence is corrupt, to the middle class as it casts a jaundiced eye on the struggles of youth to escape routine existence, to all who have lost the capacity to see that man, his thoughts, his principles, his judgments are holy—to all who see man as merely a part of an endless process of self-differentiation, the church must affirm that man is the recipient of a God whose judgment, whose word, whose constructive grace is bonded to the human condition.

Perhaps the world waits not for a word from "beings of a golden kind," but for a word from the discredited, the church. For the church, subordinate to its legacy, knows that its life is not merely a part of chaos; it knows also that its faith guarantees that civilization is more than a broken shard and that man's "making" is not debris but a holy calling.

[22] Tennessee Williams, *The Night of the Iguana* (New York: New Directions, 1961), pp. 123–124.

CHAPTER THREE

Christianity
and
Justice

Christianity is in the world and is inescapably concerned with the "making" of justice. Its understanding of the kind of justice possible must be mined from its legacy and not from the welter of theories which the world has created. As we shall see, the world, since it too is involved in "making," is not without insight. At the same time it is the task of Christianity not merely to underline but to contribute a dimension which the world cannot arrive at. Christianity need not, for instance, ally itself with either the dark realism of the Machiavellian tradition or the rich-hearted hopefulness of liberalism. The Machiavellian tradition has recognized that human justice cannot be unrelated to the security interest at the base of every power structure and the liberals have believed that man, since he is a rational and moral being, can transcend the limitations of self-interest. Those who stand outside the church must work with some such political theory. And, in doing so, they make their contributions. Each testifies to a dimension of human experience that he sees in a world unaware of what the believer knows, namely, that God's involvement in man's history has eternally changed the character of both pessimism and optimism.

In part the Christian can understand both of these traditions because the church, ignoring its legacy, has often lost itself in the world's options. The church of Gregory VII and Innocent III exercised a control of power in a way that approximated the darkest realism. At the same time no responsible Catholic thinker would seek a return to the power politics of the medieval ecclesia. In the same sense Protestantism cannot repeat itself and return to the period when it was encapsulated within the simple optimism of the social gospel. Indeed, both of these involvements have shown the church that it must develop its understanding of justice out of its own inheritance in order that it will be able to cooperate with but not be imprisoned within the world's thinking.

The Christian principle of justice rests upon the conviction that human destiny can neither be identified with God nor be separated from his healing presence. The community of faith is thus in a position to cooperate with Machiavellian realism even as it points to the unnecessary limits of that position. Simultaneously, it can cooperate with the optimism of the liberal tradition even while remaining vigilant lest the liberal tradition identify its vision with the divine.

Christianity must be very careful in establishing its position lest it select some fragment from the Bible which fits into either optimism or pessimism. One can find in the Bible admonitions which would suggest a simple moralism.

> He has showed you, O man, what is good;
>   and what does the Lord require of you
> but to do justice, and to love kindness,
>   and to walk humbly with your God?
>
> Micah 6:8

One can also find words which suggest a dark view of the possibility of justice. Pessimists are fond of quoting Jesus: "And you will hear of wars and rumors of wars; see that you are not alarmed; for this must take place for the end is not yet" (Matthew 24:6).

Although attributed to Jesus this apocalyptic admonition is still a fragment. Any particular word of Jesus selected out of the total signal of the Bible that fits too neatly into an answer may have its roots elsewhere. One can no more get inside the mind of Jesus by building on one or several of his statements than one could, by the same process, get into the mind of Shakespeare. At many points the Bible touches the position of the world and its psychology: it would have to, for it responds to all that is human. Hearts become buoyant and men hope: hearts grow heavy and men despair. But it is not the buoyant hope or the heavy despair which is the voice of the Bible.

[66]

Every fragment of the Bible must be related to that which constitutes the uniqueness of the Bible, the conviction that God declared himself to his people at Sinai and that he renewed his covenant unmistakably in Jesus.[1]

The Christian principle of justice cannot, any more than its other insights, be reduced to a formula. A formula would constitute an act of idolatry. The Christian witnesses to the explosive presence of God in the midst of the flux of life. Neither an explosion nor a flux permits formalistic solutions. In part a solution by a priori definition is prohibited because, as we have seen, God calls man to creativity, to his own "making." He must constantly "make" judgments about the world, its politics and its concern for justice. He is prohibited from adopting cynicism because to do so would be to deny God's Incarnation. He is equally denied the possibility of making any political solution into a final answer because to do so would be to destroy God's freedom and freeze him to the passing human venture.

Each Christian, taking his apprehension of the legacy seriously, must determine, with fear and trembling, the kind of cooperation that he will undertake with the world's political orders. He must always make a judg-

[1] It must be pointed out that Sinai cannot be understood as a clearly discernible historical event. What happened at Sinai cannot be measured by historical methods. Like every mountain it has a cloud around it. All that can be said historically is that from the moment of Israel's first consciousness it pointed back to a mystery which preceded its historical records, the mystery of Sinai. See Judges 5 and especially Deuteronomy 26:5–9 as a poetic apprehension of that mystery.

[67]

ment on whether political life has become idolatrous or whether it remains relatively creative.

The Christian, both related and flexible, must make a judgment about the concrete problems of contemporary society. He must come to some assessment of the political tension between the East and the West, the problems of the technological improvement of the economy, the racial inequalities that still beset man and the role of government in common life.

The dominant crisis—and having faith is being able to live with crisis—is the political, economic and perhaps military conflict between communism and the West.

Christians along with others are required to assess the creativity of two different systems of "making" justice. Unfortunately, these judgments have been made in a polemical atmosphere. In part, the insecurities of communism and capitalism have been responsible for the either/or quality of choice that has permeated the assessment. In part, men have been responsible for making human systems into false absolutes. In either case the time has come to take the judgment out of the area in which men invest their systems with ultimate and final authority. Every system, as we have suggested, is a result of man's acceptance of the task to which he has been called. No system reflects God, and every system is incomplete.

The first premise of a responsible assessment is that every system of justice must be divorced from the religious question. The Christian recognizes that, although he is related to and responsible for the system in which he operates, ultimately he must stand outside that system. From that perspective he recognizes that the difference between the Soviet Union, for instance, and the United States is the difference between a system which uproots and abuses independent religion and a system which tolerates Christianity and uses it for its own comfort. Humanly speaking there is of course a great difference, and yet both systems are outside the Christian context. Ultimately the system must be measured in terms of its "making" or creativity and not merely by its use or abuse of the Christian legacy.

The second premise is that each system must be measured in terms of its own historical possibility. With few exceptions communist nations, as they attempted their "making," did not have at their disposal a *tradition* of political democracy. The Soviet Union, China, Southeast Asia have not suppressed the tradition of the free ballot. They have merely replaced an inefficient political absolutist tradition with a relatively efficient communist bureaucracy. Indeed, the fact that both the Soviet Union and China constitute a "threat" indicates that they have been engaged in creative "making." No matter how aggravating that system may be to the West, the Christian has no alternative but to be glad that a system which once produced only serfs and coolies now produces men who can engage in high technological "making." One hopes, of course, that an easing of the cold war will provide an opportunity for dialogue so that the Western traditions of political democracy will become increasingly appealing to nations which have had little experience in that area.

At the same time America is also the victim of its own

history. A young nation, underpopulated, possessing infinite resources at the time when the industrial revolution stimulated creativity was able to engage in its "making" without the kind of planning so essential to European, including communist, states. As a result the nation has been a little gun-shy about recognizing that the community has a responsibility for its citizens, their education, their health, and their economic betterment.

Third, it must be assumed that, although every Christian operates ultimately out of his legacy, each must work within his own political system.[2] One must expect that an American Christian will be free to recognize and accept the limits of his system of justice and one must suppose the same for Christians on the other side of the iron curtain. It would be irresponsible on the part of American Christians to destroy or to weaken the courage to exist and function within a communist state. The idolatries of each system must of course be exposed, but one hopes that they will be exposed by those *within* the system. The Soviet insecurity regarding absolute control of its buffer zones exceeds the normal needs of security. No nation can be absolutely secure. Hungary and 1956 remain a bad memory. At the same time the American security system has created a Vietnam which has caused men of conscience to all but forget Hungary. The idolatries, however, must be exposed in a creative manner. The Christian must be eternally critical, but he dare not be nihilistic. There is something pathetic about the kind

[2] Obviously I presuppose that Nazism or nihilism is quite different from the communist world. In part this is because communism is international, in theory at least, free from racism and radically more creative in the use of its energies and resources.

of liberalism which takes its critique more seriously than the robustness of the human process. Again, the creed of a Christian is:

> I believe in God the father almighty.
> Maker of heaven and earth ...

One thinks of the manner in which President Lyndon B. Johnson has sometimes been made into a malevolent figure instead of being seen as, in part, the victim of a corporate quest for security. Liberalism often finds itself operating out of a darkness that exceeds even that of the Machiavellian.

From the Christian point of view there is darkness in every human venture. At the same time man is more than his failures.

Nations must create foreign policies but they need not make their foreign policies into their fate. What defines a civilized nation is its retention of the power to correct its mistakes. Civilized men take politics seriously but need not make politics into a religion. Man does not need to freeze his risky efforts to give shape to chaos. For the Christian, God can be neither bound to nor isolated from political creativity. The Christian does not give his "making" finality, nor does he consign politics to the devil.

What marks the civilized man is his ability to change his tactics to achieve his goal. The primitive man is stuck with a system of frozen taboos. But the civilized man, because he is not mechanically related to his system, is able to erase, experiment, redesign. *The civilized man never "has" justice: he is always in the process of "making" it.*

The Christian, while being critical of the deflection of creative energies into self-defeating security systems, must not allow himself to be browbeaten by his high hopes. History, inasmuch as it is, in Becker's words, more than "an endless process of self-determination," has a future.

Having suggested the perspective in which the contest between political systems must be viewed, we can now turn to our responsibility (assuming that Christians beyond the iron curtain will be attending to theirs) of lighting the darkness.

It is easy for a young nation's actions to outrun its wisdom. Reversing our historical orientation toward isolation we have sought to achieve international responsibility by becoming the world's policeman. Our inflexible stance in Southeast Asia would indicate that we have confused our policies with the revelation at Sinai. Our reluctance, over the last decade, to treat with revolutionary movements indicates that we are not sure that Asia should have much of a voice in the shaping of its future.

Nations have an extraordinary capacity for deceiving themselves and we may have entered upon a new form of imperialism. That we are not primarily interested in economic gain does not mean that we will not be guilty of imposing more controls than is our right. The Roman empire was able to function not merely because Rome needed the grain of the ancient world but because it believed that it had been called to save the Mediterranean world from banditry. There may not be much difference between the *Pax Romana* and the *Pax Americana*.

The church cannot subscribe to the view that all policies are valid if they serve the national interest. In a complex and interrelated world the appeal to self-interest merely leads to chaos. At the same time the church cannot expect the nation, in one dramatic act of *mea culpa*, to reverse its position. Only with patience and firmness can the church press beyond the positions of Machiavellianism and liberalism. Both are bankrupt.

All our energies cannot go into the solution of our foreign-policy problems. The technological changes that automation promises require a new assessment of man's nature.

Both man's experience and the Bible point to the uniqueness of man. Like the animal world he is a part of nature. He is subject to its laws. Unlike the animal world, however, he has been able to understand those laws and to use them to make himself in some sense independent of nature. He is not dependent upon the limited harvest that nature provides. By readjusting the environment he is able to force nature to surrender a vast richness of food that nature on its own was unwilling to give. Man is more than nature: he is its master.

His lordship has been expressed in his ingenuity and in his understanding of the structure of nature. Herein is his advantage. The relationship between man and nature is not reciprocal. Nature cannot understand man but man can understand nature.

Man's road from early slavery to mastery was long and arduous. The invention of the wheel, smelting and fashioning of metals, steam, gasoline, electricity and atomic energy have given him the power to create machines which enable him to create vast and complicated civilizations with far less expenditure of personal energy than was possible for the early caveman. Each new victory over nature has three phases. First is the conquest itself, the invention of the new instrument or process. Second, man faces the problem of his attitude toward both the invention and the changes that it creates. Third, he discovers that the invention which solves old problems also creates new ones. Man may be a lord, but his lordship is never static and never secure.

The problem of automation also follows this pattern. Once by simple machines man himself fashioned the articles that he produced. When the factory introduced production through an assembly line, the individual's responsibility for a complete product disappeared. By creating more complicated machines man eliminated the necessity of direct confrontation with the product. The only employee who ever sees a whole car is the one who removes it from the assembly line and puts it in storage. The assembly line separated man from the product and made him a part of the process.

Automation represents the next logical step from the assembly line. A fully automated factory would remove man even further from the product. Whereas the assembly line separated him from the total product and confronted him only with the part, automation separates him also from the part and confronts him only with the machine that makes the part.

Automation is a stage in man's history. It is no more

an option that he can accept or reject than was the invention of the wheel or the steam engine. What man faces, therefore, is not the choice of whether or not there will be automation, but his attitude toward the new process and the new problems created by that process.

Two attitudes prohibit man from giving automation the welcome that it deserves. His pleasure in automation is corrupted by a philosophy and by a fear. Man was called to be civilized, to be a "maker." However, he resists civilization because his inertia (sin?) causes him to prefer a less challenging adversary. Either he makes an idol out of the less complicated past or he makes one out of nature. He orients himself toward simplicity. When he does so, he finds it difficult to trust the machine. Handwork seems to him to be the natural way to make something. The machine, it seems to him, turns man into a robot. The logic of this rather simple naturalism can be seen in the following critique of industrialism cited by John Kouwenhoven:

> A man and his family are no longer, even in the country, a self-sufficient community, living close to a stable tradition and the processes of nature, but are mobile, isolated, rootless atoms, dependent upon a multitude of external agencies. Unless he makes a determined effort, an effort that invites the label of eccentricity, modern man loses the use of his hands and his feet and his senses, not to mention the time and capacity for reflection.

Kouwenhoven goes on to take issue with this simple-minded naturalism.

[75]

What does it mean to say that man's life in pre-industrial society was "natural," while the life of man today is not? Is it not "natural" for man to make tools, and to power those tools with machines, and to use those tools to remake his environment? What is "unnatural" about being mobile? Were we not born with legs and endowed by nature with minds capable of conceiving of the wheel and a motor to drive it? Is mobility on wheels less "natural" than mobility on legs, or only less brutish and more "human"? And what is unnatural about a rootless atom? Could there be anything more unnatural than an atom *with* roots? Are a man and his family who have television, a car, and a telephone really more "isolated" than those who herded sheep in Palestine two thousand years ago, or those who lived in eighteenth-century English country houses? Are stable traditions more natural than unstable ones? And are the processes of nature, to which we like to think of being close, really stable or, as Werner Heisenberg's "uncertainty principle" in modern physics suggests, at best relatively so? And isn't it curious that a society which has deprived all but the eccentric of the use of their feet and hands and senses, regularly cracks the four minute mile, buys fishing rods and skis in unprecedented quantities, operates turret lathes and typewriters with dextrous grace, and has learned to respond creatively to sensory stimuli which, without the microscopes and X rays and other resources, technology and science have put at our disposal, man would never have seen or felt or heard?

In short, are not all of those deprecatory comparisons of the "natural" life of the old days with the "unnatural" life of our own society either meaningless or—worse—a sentimental refuge from thinking about the challenge which our society really offers us? For there is

[76]

a challenge involved, as there always has been and always will be.[3]

Clear thinking must save us from escaping from the challenge of the present. It is sinful to measure the present by the past. While the assembly line cannot rival handwork as to quality, it can flood the common life with materials which change man from a burden-carrying donkey to a thinking human being. The handcrafted Rolls Royce can never be reduplicated on the Detroit assembly line, but then the Rolls factory cannot provide cheap and available transportation for the multitude.

It has been argued by the naturalists that the submersion of the worker in the assembly line frustrates his happiness. That kind of happiness is an illusion. *There never has been an economic system which can make men happy.* The underpaid crofters making their Harris tweed in the Hebrides are no more joyful than the workers on the line. One rarely sees the nearly blind Belgian lace workers dancing happily down the street. The process of automation is not only not "unnatural" but is actually natural to the life of that man who is not a part of nature but is its lord.

Automation is a valid step only if it increases man's lordship, if it demands of him a higher skill and imagination. But that is precisely what automation does do. The assembly line was only a first step. Drudgery, except as part of the process to something better, cannot be defended. When the fully automated factory emerges, man

[3] Kouwenhoven, *The Beer Can by the Highway* (Garden City, N.Y.: Doubleday & Co.), pp. 93–95.

[77]

will be introduced to a new level of challenge and freedom. Before man had tamed the animals and invented the machine, he himself had to do the work of animals and machines. The early steps in a machine economy, nonautomated factories, gave him only a limited freedom. When automation arrives, the machine will accomplish the assembly-line drudgery that man once did. Then and only then will he be master.

The vision of human freedom through automation has been persuasively stated by Sir Leon Bagrit, chairman of Elliot-Automation, Ltd.

> Your mind has to be adequately cultivated and your body has to be adequately developed. This is the concept which the Greeks had, too. But the high level reached by the Greeks was only possible because the routine dulling work was done by slaves. Today, if we use the slave service of automation intelligently and courageously, we have the chance of building a really high civilization for ourselves. I mean for the whole community, not just for a small elite on the Greek pattern.[4]

The problems that automation creates are twofold. They are the human problems of temporary unemployment and the cultural problem of greater leisure. A compassionate civilization must see to it that the human hardships involved in automation are kept to a minimum. All the resources of the nation must assist in the retraining and re-educational program which will enable an army of unskilled and semiskilled workers to become

[4] *New York Herald-Tribune*, Paris ed., December 23, 1964, p. 10.

the masters of the vast machinery which they will install and service. In a nation which has been as successful as America at mass education, that will not be an insurmountable problem. Actually the machine itself, especially if it is complicated, is a mind-stretching experience. So long as we lived in a "hand-and-broom" economy there was little to stimulate the intellect. The necessity of mastering the machine will stimulate the intellect and challenge the imagination. Men who can tend an automated factory will no longer be satisfied with the dull leisure that characterized the days of machine slavery. *The greatest task before us will not be technological training but the creation of a mass culture which will excite the mind and the imagination.* The greatest jolt will not come to the workers and managers. It will come to writers, playwrights and musicians as they face men whose minds will be too critical to accept the mediocrity which is peddled to men who are still treated as dumb beasts or unthinking machines and not yet as lords.

More aggravating than the psychological changes which automation requires is the spiritual adjustment necessary to complete the social and economic transformation of our racially divided society. Happily, the anguish through which the nation has lived for over a century is now being resolved in part through legislation. The Civil Rights Act of 1965 has enabled the nation to turn the corner and, although much remains to be done, the movement toward full equality is now irreversible.

The problem remaining is largely psychological. More

than he is prepared to admit the white man is the victim of his own experience. Only peripherally related to the inner world of the Negro, the liberal white man imagined that the belated legislation would be gratefully received and that it would create the opportunity for genuine communication and good will. That did not happen. To the white man the Negro seemed unnecessarily impatient because he did not receive all that he wanted in one quick action and to the Negro even the rectification which legislation helped to create seemed paternalistic. Scars that were created over a century are not so easily erased and, like the Irish and the English, the Negro is in a situation in which he cannot seem to forget and the white man is in one in which he would rather not remember.

The white man, operating out of his suburban ghetto, is content with one slow step at a time. The Negro, still facing the heavy backlog of educational and economic disadvantages, finds it difficult to be pleasantly grateful. The Black Power movement, especially a problem to liberals who have fought for the Negro for generations, is the inevitable result of the Negro being transformed from a grateful sponge to an aggressive defender of his own rights. While aggression is surely not the final solution, the sensitive Christian must recognize that it is nevertheless the indispensable first step toward maturity. Just as an adolescent rebels rudely against the controls of his parents before he becomes an adult, just as the Chinese have had to become aggressive as they revolted against colonialism, so too must every minority have the right to insist that virtue based upon paternalism, even liberal paternalism, does not provide full equality. The Negro knows, as the sensitive Christian should know, that the Negro will be unable to accept the white man until he is able to compete with the white man in all the ranges of their common civilization.

The problem is a difficult one but there is no basis for cynicism. A combination of patience and contrition cannot help but create the atmosphere in which the Negro will both receive and act out of full citizenship. No sensitive person, as one hopes the white man will be, has the right to ignore his tragic and guilty past. But that past arises only out of human imperfection: it is not determined. Indeed, the Christian knows that the power of darkness is limited and that there is an assurance that, once true equality is achieved, genuine community will materialize. The grace of God is on the side of civilization.

Matthew Arnold in *Culture and Anarchy* was profoundly right in seeing that the middle class was the source of morality. And indeed the middle class has become the accomplice of Christianity. But an accomplice is often a dangerous friend and Christianity has allowed itself to be shaped by the virtues of middle-class existence. Conspicuous in that morality was a suspicion of strong government.

Civilization, that unique marriage of freedom and order, is constantly threatened by one or the other of two political diseases. The first disease, the omnistate, throws

[81]

away freedom in order to create an iron order. The second disease, the nonstate, throws away order that it may preserve freedom. It is difficult to imagine which is worse —a government that attempts to solve all of man's problems, or a government that is unable or unwilling to solve any of them.

The omnistate and the nonstate are related even though they are in opposition. In the modern world the nonstate has been the forerunner of the omnistate. Communism has not been able to take over in any country where the state met its problems while preserving freedom. Communism has made little inroads in states like Sweden and Austria, where the state represents a middle ground. The disciples of the nonstate are critical of Sweden because it engages in too much planning. The communists are critical of a state like Austria because it permits too much freedom. But the courage to combine freedom and order leads toward the complexity of civilization. The simple logic which demands *either* freedom or order, and assumes that they are not compatible, is uncivilized.

It is unfortunate that the prevailing concept of the state in America has been called "the welfare state." "Welfare state" suggests that the government from Roosevelt through Johnson has been verging on the omnistate. Nothing could be further from the truth. The American political climate is closer to the middle way of Sweden than it is to the simple way of either the omnistate of communism or what was the virtually nonstate concept of some of the oriental nations. The genius of

American politics is that it has avoided extremes in order to do justice to the complex human need. The word that best describes the American political climate is "mixed." A more philosophical word would be "pragmatism." By pragmatism we mean the opposite of any doctrinaire theory or principle. Pragmatists are committed to an idea only if it works. Because the omnistate doesn't work, and because the lazy state only prepares the way for communism, America, one hopes, has committed itself to a state providing for a delicate balance between governmental power and the freedom of the citizenry. In election after election the people have insisted that a government is required which provides answers without being despotic. One would no more want a government that controlled all of life than one would want a government that was insensitive to the responsibility of leadership. Happily, America has had governments which, broadly speaking, have been both responsible and restrained.

One can be sure of the political health of the American people so long as they reject a philosophy which insists that the choice is simply between order and freedom. So long as the people avoid thinking in a formula, so long as they accept the fact that all true creativity must be mixed, one may be sure that American civilization will be responsive and sensitive to human needs. A welfare state is not wanted if that description means an omnistate (and it never has in the mind of any American president), but a welfare state is desired if it means that the nation will continue to stumble forward as human beings by interlacing the responsible powers of business, labor and government.

Because the Christian recognizes that civilization constitutes the most complex form of "making" to which God has called him, he must take seriously every problem of justice.

The Christian must forever walk a tightrope. He can neither isolate himself from the political ambiguities of life or pretend that his solution to those ambiguities constitutes true justice. Walking a tightrope is a dangerous and often a lonely task.

He dare not become cynical, for to do so would be to deny the darkness to which the gospel is a constant answer.

The Christian must help to create solutions, but he may not pretend that those solutions are either final or free from error.

He must commit himself deeply to politics but be careful lest his politics become his church.

We do not have a just society. Nor are we exempt from the responsibility of creating new—however imperfect—forms of justice. Even if we fail we must provide answers. We are not repelled by our system, nor do we worship it. We serve it by criticizing it and improving it.

We have every reason to be grateful for our lot. Our "impure" society is still healthy. It is not a just society and yet it takes justice seriously. Of such is the kingdom of heaven.

CHAPTER FOUR

Christianity
Civilization
and Sex

The health of a civilization is in part defined by its ability to blend flesh and spirit creatively. The depersonalization of human sexuality, through an exaggerated emphasis on either flesh or spirit, marks the decay of a civilization.

American civilization in its recent past has been threatened by the false spirituality of Victorian moralism: it now faces an equally dangerous distortion, the reduction of man to a glandular morality. Victorian morality by and large viewed sex as a necessary but nevertheless lower part of man's life. The naturalist's reaction against the Victorians tends to view sex not only as central but as the very foundation of personality.

Christianity cannot support either the view that man

is pure spirit or that he is mere animal. Theology must criticize every distortion so that man will be enabled to receive himself in the full complexity of his civilized existence.

The middle classes, the heirs of Victorianism, are confused and shocked by the revolution in contemporary sex practices and attitudes. The old standards of chastity and fidelity seem to have given way to a concept of instant and occasional sex. To make matters worse, accepted mores no longer seem to be limited to heterosexuality. Homosexuality, through the writings of men like James Baldwin and Tennessee Williams, seems to have become an honorable estate.

Although Christianity, sociologically speaking, is a largely middle-class movement, the Christian thinker must not allow himself to be seduced by a sense of moral outrage.

Contemporary sexual relativism, no matter how dangerous it may be to individuals, must be understood as an inevitable protest against the rigidities of an earlier Victorian morality. Christianity, in committing itself too easily to a prudish sexual morality, is itself partly responsible for the modern temper. To the argument between the sexual relativist and the traditionalist the Christian must be an interested observer. Both represent an attempt by man to "make" a meaningful order out of sexual chaos. Christianity cannot identify itself with any "making" but must encourage the purification and the clarification of every order.

The Christian will be assisted in his achievement of

sympathetic objectivity if he remembers that biblical man had an understanding of sexual existence which was radically different from the positions taken in the contemporary debate. For biblical man sexuality is understood neither as a necessary repression nor as a means of redemption. In the Old Testament, men and women married, produced children. They did so with a kind of innocence which was threatened as biblical man moved out of his protected culture into the chaos of the Gentile world. When this happened, in the period of the New Testament, sex became something that modern man can understand, a problem.

There can be little doubt but that the New Testament tends to minimize sexual existence. There were several reasons why St. Paul could make so outrageous a statement as "it is better to marry than to burn." In part, many of the leaders of the early church, including Paul, were itinerants whose vocation made marriage difficult and who, as a result, had little experience with such a relationship. In part, the early church was radically apocalyptic in its psychology. Expecting a literal ending of normal history they had little reason to support or even to understand the rhythms and structures necessary to a continuing civilization.

But more importantly the early church was boxed in by participating in a real tension between its views of personality and views refracted from the pagan world.

Without rehearsing the extended literature which historical Christianity has created on the subject of sexual morals, it is useful to point out that Christianity placed itself on the side of the sexual discipline because its task, as a missionary religion, was to speak not with an abstract definition but to the pagan world. From the viewpoint of the biblical world, paganism was evil not because it was the world—the Bible also was within the world—but because it was a world grossly out of balance. Although the Hollywood picture of Roman orgies is surely exaggerated, nevertheless there is little doubt that sexual vitality was often uncontrolled by a strong sense of sexual responsibility. The medieval emphasis on virginity, including the magnification of Mary, was in part Christianity's response to pagan excess. The adulation of Mary was the inevitable and perhaps necessary corrective to a world in whose judgment the rights of Joseph, as the husband, far outweighed the vision of the Madonna. The elevation of virginity provided Western man with an alternative to a sexual freedom which was more animal than human. All to whom promiscuity represents an abandonment of civilization and its values are debtors to the tradition of the Virgin.

Just as the Virgin provided a symbol for the correction of a particular form of sexual instability so has the modern man formed a correction for the overspiritualization which the cult of the Virgin helped to create. And the Christian must constantly keep in mind that the present sexual revolution, chaotic as it may seem, is not so much a final answer as it is part of the process by which man finds a meaningful answer. Computers may come to their conclusions easily and quickly but man matures only through the pain of endless debate and continuous modification.

D. H. Lawrence, a tortured religious writer, provided modern man with an antidote madonna, Lady Chatterley. Lady Chatterley, as all readers of *Lady Chatterley's Lover* know, found freedom from a sexually sterile marriage by entering into an illicit and ecstatic relationship with her gardener. Gradually emancipated, Lady Chatterley became, as D. H. Lawrence saw it, a free and exciting person in her sexual activities. She not only enjoyed the relationship, but through the loss of all inhibition she was transformed into a free soul.

Whether or not D. H. Lawrence's book is an abiding work of art is not the question. Whether or not the words extended the artistic vision or merely contributed to Lawrence's psychological therapy is not the problem. Nor need one concern oneself, at the moment, with Lawrence's tendency to minimize sexuality by virtually equating male and female. What is most to be remembered is that Lawrence was not peddling pornography, that he too was engaged in creative "making." Lawrence was attempting a blend of spirit and flesh which visualized man as liberated but which did not equate that liberation with pure biology. In the end it is Mellors, the gardener, who communicates that man cannot be fulfilled in fornication.

> I've no business to take a woman into my life, unless my life does something and gets somewhere, inwardly at least, to keep us both fresh. A man must offer a woman *some* meaning in his life, if it's going to be an isolated life, and if she's a genuine woman. I can't be just your male concubine.[1]

[1] D. H. Lawrence, *Lady Chatterley's Lover* (New York: Grove Press, 1957), p. 345.

In this sentence Lawrence makes possible the synthesis of the two madonnas. Man is spirit as well as flesh, flesh as well as spirit. And it is out of this combination that civilization must "make" its structure of sexual meaning.

The modern man may not be as imaginative as was D. H. Lawrence. His self-indulgence tempts him to separate the madonnas. He is sensitive to the distortions within the Mary cult; he is less likely to see that a correction may itself be an incomplete answer.

Neither madonna solves the whole problem. Each is a partial answer. The Virgin corrected irresponsible sensualism and Lady Chatterley corrected prudishness. One need not waste time by pitting one madonna against the other. Whether there were more dangers in the contempt for sex which the Virgin cult produced or more dangers in Lady Chatterley's apparent glorification of sex is a useless question, because there is nothing to be said for either the contempt or the glorification. Ultimately the adherents of either cult were, and are, unable to understand and express their sexual existence on a fully human level.

Why? Because each symbol taken literally is grotesque. Every faith uses images and all literature uses transpositions. When a cartoonist creates a mouse who behaves like a human being a transposition takes place. It is amusing to see an animal struggle with a problem which is not natural to him. It is even amusing to see him, after a fashion, succeed. Similarly one enjoys seeing bears ride bicycles in a circus. Likewise one can enjoy the picture of an angelic being trying to adapt himself to the limitations of human existence. It might be amusing to see an angel cope with traffic, bureaucracy, or income tax returns. It is not, however, amusing to see the situation reversed. One is not pleased to see a man pretend to be an angel, and the sight of a man behaving as an animal is distasteful. Human existence is centered in humanity. One is awed, pleased or amused to see the nonhuman become human. One is depressed and frightened when the human is depreciated, and human beings try to engage in either a "higher" or a "lower" activity. Men and women are dehumanized if the madonna is either too refined or too coarse.

Man is the only being who is a mystery to himself. He cannot be an animal. And, as we saw in the preceding chapter, he cannot be a machine. For both an animal and a machine live on one level of existence. Both live only in time. Neither has an intimation of immortality or eternity. Neither the animal nor the machine experiences guilt or humor or has the capacity to accept criticism. Only the being who can laugh, who can feel the sting of guilt and who can participate in a double dimension is capable of civilized existence. The Madonna and Lady Chatterley must be seen as groping and confused attempts to understand the human situation. Both failed because they were too simple and too one-sided to do justice to man's complexity, a complexity which requires a blending of flesh and spirit.

What then is the Christian contribution to the understanding of man as a sexual being? The Christian must both maintain his freedom from endorsing a fixed cultural solution and recognize that civilized man can achieve his answer only through the process of debate. The Christian, as we have said, must resist the seduction of middle-class outrage, and he must simultaneously resist identifying the church with contemporary sexual experimentalism. It is his task to remind man that he has no fixed answer, that he is in the process of searching one out. Man, from the Christian point of view, is always a "maker" and a searcher. He may stumble but he is not demonic.

Clearly, then, Christianity cannot identify itself with traditional solutions to the chaos of sex. Christianity and middle-class morality are not synonymous. The institution of marriage, with its legal and social buttresses,[2] is not a Christian institution. It was man, not God, who created monogamy, and that[3] concept must be measured as human, not as divine.[4]

That the institution of marriage is a human construction, that it must constantly be subjected to criticism, does not mean, as we shall see, that it is necessarily ex-

[2] It would be disingenuous of this writer to pretend that as an individual he has not been shaped by his own middle-class existence.

[3] Catholics, for whom marriage is a sacrament, must of course disagree.

[4] Many attempts have been made by Christians to ground the sexuality within the obligatory character of monogamy. But, in view of the silence of the Bible (and the creedal summaries of the Bible) all such arguments seem to be based upon special pleading. At most, one can determine that the spirit of the Bible requires that a man be personal. Whether in marriage or out he is prohibited from exploiting other persons.

pendable. There is a tendency, once institutions are separated from a transcendental authority, to assume with the empiricists that all is an "endless process of differentiation." But that dogmatic view minimizes the creative power of the human. It may be that monogamous marriage, like democracy, represents an insight into the enduring greatness of man as a creator.

In any case the problem of sexuality cannot be solved by either depressing man out of civilization and making him into a complicated animal or by elevating him out of civilization and making him into an abstraction.

Modern man is faced by two such temptations. Each would allow him to escape a fully civilized solution. The first is the escape through primitivism and the second is an escape through abstract thinking. We turn first to Freud and second to the contextual, or situational ethic.

The sharpest attack upon the rigidities of middle-class moralism has come from the insights of Sigmund Freud. Freud has communicated an important understanding of the intensity and centrality of the sexual drive. He thus corrects medieval attempts to see man as a primarily rational and spiritual being.

Let us begin by accepting the general thrust of Freud's insight that man is a libidinal creature. Humanity is enriched by recognizing that a child's need cannot be dissociated from his need for gratification. The journey through the oral, anal, and genital areas may be overstructured but, in the main, man cannot be dissociated from a conception of security which is related to pleasure. All are further indebted to an understanding of biological man by recognizing that he possesses an unconscious, a prerational source of energy whose anatomy can be divided into the id, the ego and the superego.

Christianity cannot quarrel with a psychology which is grounded in biology and therefore illuminates man's rootage in nature. Nor can Christianity quarrel with the notion that an element of human existence, the id, is totally directed toward pleasure, totally indifferent to morality. Pleasure is as valid a dimension as responsibility.

Christianity must raise questions, however, about the implications of Freud's thought which diminish man's capacity to understand that he is a civilized as well as a libidinal being. At this point the critical thinker must recognize that Freud is limited not because he is biological but because he fails to do justice to man as more than biological. Like all heirs of rationalism Freud allows his method to overleap its bounds. Or as John Macquarrie says:

> The major criticism of naturalism, however, is that it involves us in a gigantic one-sided abstraction. It takes a segment of experience—the segment which is amenable to measurement and analysis—and represents it as the entire reality.[5]

Although Freud did concern himself with culture, especially in *The Future of an Illusion* and in *Civilisation and Its Discontents* he "summarily rejected anthropological findings which would contradict his theories."[6]

[5] John Macquarrie, *Twentieth Century Religious Thought* (New York: Harper & Row, 1963), p. 112.
[6] Clara Thompson, *Psychoanalysis, Evolution and Theory* (New York: Hermitage House, 1950), p. 135.

The failure to take civilization as a trans-biological dimension was intensified by the fact that Freud built his psychology around germinal and not mature experience. Culture is defined only from the point of view of the child's reception of authority. Thus civilization is locked into the anatomy of the superego.

> The superego is the representative in the personality of the traditional values and ideals of society as they are handed down from parents to children. In this connexion it should be borne in mind that the child's superego is not a reflection of the parents' conduct but rather of the parents' superegos. An adult may say one thing and do another, but it is what he says, backed up by threats or gifts, that counts in the shaping of the child's ethical standards. In addition to the parents, other agents of society take a hand in the formation of the child's superego. Teachers, ministers, policemen—in fact anyone who is in a position of authority over the child may function in the role of parents. The child's reactions to these figures of authority are largely determined, however by what he has assimilated from his parents. What purpose does the superego serve? Primarily it serves the purpose of controlling and regulating those impulses whose uncontrolled expression would endanger the stability of society.[7]

Civilization and its order seen from the point of view of an adult invites dialogue between the individual and the cultural modality; seen from the point of view of a child that modality can only be intimidating.

Freud's problem is that his attempt to defend civilization, as in his essay *Civilisation and Its Discontents*, is

[7] Hall, *Primer of Freudian Psychology* (New York: New American Library), p. 34.

constantly corrupted by the fact that the self is manacled to the pleasure principle. The priority and authority of that principle insures that civilization will be understood restrictively rather than creatively.

> If civilisation imposes such great sacrifices not only on man's sexuality but on his aggressivity, we can understand better why it is hard for him to be happy in that civilisation. In fact, primitive man was better off in knowing no restrictions of instinct. . . . Civilised man has exchanged a portion of his possibilities of happiness for a portion of security.[8]

Freud's thought is almost as divisive as was that of a second century theologian. "What indeed," Tertullian said, "has Athens to do with Jerusalem? What concord is there between the Academy and the Church?"[9] The polarization of pleasure and civilization warrants that Freud will end with something less than a clear defense of civilization.

> For a wide variety of reasons, it is very far from my intention to express an opinion upon the value of human civilisation. . . . One thing only do I know for certain and that is that man's judgments of value follow directly his wishes for happiness—that accordingly, they are an attempt to support his illusions with arguments. . . . Thus I have not the courage to rise up above my fellow men as a prophet, and I bow to their reproach that I can offer them no consolation: for at bottom that is

[8] Sigmund Freud, *Civilisation and Its Discontents*, trans. by James Strachey (New York: W. W. Norton, 1961), p. 62.

[9] *The Ante-Nicene Fathers*, vol. III, ed. by Roberts and Donaldson, trans. by Peter Holmes (Buffalo, N.Y.: The Christian Literature Publishing Company, 1885), p. 246.

what they are all demanding—the wildest revolutionaries no less passionately than the most virtuous believers.[10]

And so Freud leaves man grasping but doomed because every definition of purpose becomes merely a deflection from the primitive foundation out of which the self operates. In the end Freud has undermined man's confidence and courage to be a "maker" of his own sexual order. Where Christianity and Freud differ is that the Christian is much more sympathetic to man's attempt to achieve a definition, a civilized framework for his chaos.

Whatever the limits, and they are many, of the middle-class attempt to control sexuality those limits do represent an attempt of a human culture to fulfill its obligation. Robert Lowell, who also appreciated the limits of a Puritan tradition, understood the grandeur of man and his "making" when he said:

> Yet they gave darkness some control
> and left a loophole for the soul.[11]

Freud, by deprecating human creativity, failed to leave a loophole for the soul.

We can now turn from the escape through primitivism to the escape through abstraction, the contextual ethic.

The contextual, or as it is sometimes called the situational, ethic, like Freudianism, diverts man from his task of taking civilization and "making" seriously. Whereas

[10] Freud, op. cit., pp. 91–92.
[11] Robert Lowell, "Waking Early Sunday Morning." From Near the Ocean (New York: Farrar, Straus & Giroux, Inc., 1967), p. 18.

[97]

Freudianism mires man in primitivism, the contextual ethic propels him above the traditions which shaped him. The Freudian man is fulfilled through gratification: the contextual man is fulfilled through a strategy of love.[12] But that strategy, as we shall see, is disengaged from the fabric of historical existence.

Among Protestants the contextual ethic takes two somewhat different forms. Paul Lehmann's *Ethics in a Christian Context* expresses the conviction that ethics must arise out of *koinonia* as it is understood by Reformation and nonsectarian theology. Paul Lehmann brilliantly recovers a dying tradition and suggests a new relevance for a historical ethic. However, it is his involvement with a historical modality which keeps the book from being a defense of a contextual ethic in the usual sense of the term. Joseph Fletcher, author of *Situation Ethics*, thinks that the *koinonia* basis clouds the issue and that the contextual ethic ought to arise out of a *general* concern for love.[13] Paul Lehmann, on the other hand, specifically rejects the general. "The contextual character of Christian ethics is not derived from an application to the Christian *koinonia* of a general theory of contextualism."[14]

The *koinonia* ethic is not therefore an invitation to abstraction: it is rather an illustration of how theology can take a modality of the past and interpret it imagina-

[12] Fletcher, *op. cit.*, p. 31.
[13] *Ibid.*, p. 155.
[14] Lehmann, *Ethics in a Christian Context* (New York: Harper & Row, 1963), pp. 14–15.

[98]

tively. Paul Lehmann is one of the few American theologians who take the reformation tradition seriously. From the point of view of these essays, however, he is too Protestant. While he is always fair to an Aristotle or an Aquinas he is too much concerned with putting such systems into *contest* with the Reformation to recognize that they also represent significant "making." What one misses in his thinking is the recognition that an independent civilization must be a witness not to God or the orders of creation but to the creativity to which God called man when He set him on his journey. His theology shows the relevance of the tradition but not the integrity of the world which stands outside that tradition. In any case he is not contextual, which Joseph Fletcher is. Fletcher is so situation-minded that he cannot bring himself to make a judgment about patriotic prostitution[15] while Paul Lehmann boldly uses the structure of *koinonia* to establish boundaries for a sexual ethic. "In such a context, promiscuity and prostitution simply have no place. They are *ab initio* sexual deviations."[16]

Fletcher, on the other hand, creates an atmosphere for ethics which depends upon neither revelation nor the moral composition of *koinonia*. He sees the situation ethic as an alternative to legalism and antinomianism.

> The situationist enters every decision-making situation fully armed with the ethical maxims of his community and its heritage, and he treats them with respect as illuminators of his problems. Just the same he is prepared

[15] Fletcher, *op. cit.*, p. 164.
[16] Lehmann, *op. cit.*, p. 138.

in any situation to compromise them or set them aside *in the situation* if love seems better served by doing so.[17]

At first glance this definition seems to be a fair statement about the way in which any historical individual tries to be personal rather than doctrinal amidst the ambiguities of a pluralistic culture. No man has a right to hold his tradition in a way that is offensive to another. Thus Paul said: "Then let us no more pass judgment on one another, but rather decide never to put a stumbling-block or hindrance in the way of a brother" (Romans 14:13).

At the same time where history and cultural forms are taken seriously it would be an embarrassment in personal relations if one discovered that another was forced for the sake of that relationship to violate a tradition that he loved. Indeed, being civilized means that one cares about the other's traditions and does everything possible to permit him to express them gracefully. An inherited legacy is not, as Fletcher seems to think, a dimension that one is free to omit or to bring into the situation. *Tradition is itself psychologically integral to the situation.*

Actually Fletcher only *mentions* the heritage in his definition. He never discusses it in detail in his illustrative cases. Indeed one gains the impression that the man that he is talking about is actually disengaged from a living tradition either because it has lost its meaning or because some apocalyptic crisis has divorced him from the kind of life in which tradition can be lived.

[17] Fletcher, *op. cit.*, p. 26.

Indeed his failure to take civilization and its modalities seriously explains his penchant for bizarre illustrations. His situation ethics seems to involve individuals who are either being attacked by hostile Indians or who are involved in high-level espionage or who are facing the chaos of an invading army. What such illustrations have to do with the ordinary problems of personal relationships is hard to determine. How a girl or a boy for whom a religious tradition is meaningful relates that tradition to the sexual jungle of college life is not readily discernible.

The eccentricity of the illustrations makes one suspect that Fletcher's characters lack true historical coloration: they are traditionless people. If, on the other hand, one introduces historical man, then the conception of context changes because individuals who are involved with the living past cannot live entirely in the situation, the empty present. What about war? The abstract man, if he has any sensitivity, may face the ambiguity of war without any pressure toward a traditional answer. But what if that man is not an abstraction? What if he is a Quaker? Is he as free as the floater to be ambiguous? Is an Orthodox Jew as free as a Reform Jew to be ambiguous about the Torah? Is a Roman Catholic as free as a Protestant to make a decision which is independent of or in violation of the tradition? Is it not part of the context of the Catholic in every situation that he must be obedient to his bishop? Indeed, one gains the impression that contextuality as Fletcher sees it is applicable only for the man for whom the past is no longer living. And that man as we have seen earlier is not fully a man, since he is merely involved in "the endless process of differentiation" (Becker).

If it is the obligation of Christianity to underwrite man's courage to create cultural forms, situational ethics as Fletcher defines it is as useless to our understanding of civilization as the Freudian primitivism. And when tradition is erased because it ceases to be an ingredient in the situation, inevitably one will be observing only papier-mâché figures. Look at the following illustration, which Fletcher calls "sacrificial adultery." At the end of World War II a German mother is deported to a Soviet prisoner-of-war camp. The only way that she can return home is through pregnancy.

> She turned things over in her mind and finally asked a friendly Volga German camp guard to impregnate her, which he did. Her condition being medically verified, she was sent back to Berlin and her family. They welcomed her with open arms, even when she told them how she had managed it. When the child was born, they loved him more than all the rest, on the view that little Dietrich had done more for them than anybody.[18]

Now Christianity does have an answer to extramarital relations. That answer in terms of its legacy is forgiveness, and if Hosea's experience means anything the Christian knows that when life breaks down it can, where there is grace, be reconstituted. But Fletcher's tale is not about forgiveness. Instead he is persuaded that an extramarital sexual relationship can be a tool for a higher social purpose. Perhaps, but in the course of the

[18] *Ibid.*, p. 165.

story the reader has a high sense of unreality. What about the German guard? Was he a neutral figure or did the woman not also have some responsibility for him? Was she so fertile that one tight-lipped encounter provided her with her answer? Or did the achievement of pregnancy create a living relationship? What about the child? Was he not being used and would he not have a vacuum within him as he thought about his father? None of these questions is answered as Fletcher reduces the drama of life to a pragmatic act. Surely a novelist would find more tragedy and poignancy in such a story. Clearly the situation ethics reduces life to a problem of surface engineering.

But we would not have such an appeal to surface description if Fletcher took historical and dramatic man more seriously. Unlike Professor Lehmann, who swims against the tide and attempts to reconstitute a modality of the past, Fletcher is a victim of the failure of nerve which characterizes our empiricist civilization.

One suspects that situation ethics is not only the child of empiricism but also the nephew of existentialism. Existentialism, that late child of Protestantism, emptied history of meaning. It was Kierkegaard who declared that eighteen centuries of the church's life "are in the moment of decision worth precisely nothing to the individual subject."[19] And if that legacy is worth precisely nothing it is so because "Christianity is spirit, spirit is

[19] Kierkegaard, *Concluding Unscientific Postscript*, trans. by David F. Swenson (Princeton: Princeton University Press, 1941), p. 47.

inwardness, inwardness is subjectivity, subjectivity is essentially passion, and in its maximum an infinite, personal, passionate interest in one's eternal happiness."[20]

Empiricism, Freudianism, contextualism form an unholy alliance to isolate man from the possibility of believing that his creativity is important. Empiricism reduces him to whirl, Freudianism reduces him to biology and contexualism reduces him to an abstraction by the process of isolating him from his tradition.

Christianity neither makes culture divine nor sees culture as mere debris. Thus at this point theology must be most dialectical. It must neither absolutize the human nor deny man his grandeur. As the Christian thinker turns his attention to the institution of marriage he must recognize that man as well as God is a truly creative being and that his creations do not necessarily belong to drift and decay.

Our first assumption, therefore, is that the organization of man's sexual life belongs inexorably to his destiny. The complicated order of marriage with its property rights, human rights, and responsibility for children requires definition by civilization and would so require if there were no church. Although laws never completely reflect justice, the community must constantly make laws as it, for instance, protects the rights of those who are the innocent products of sexuality. The church can no more endorse social and moral nihilism than it can endorse social and moral tyranny.

The church believes not only that a civilization may

[20] *Ibid.*, p. 33.

[104]

order its life but that it must. At the same time, since the state must be neither an omnistate nor a nonstate, it should not only create an order but also be sufficiently sensitive to process so that that order and its laws can be constantly instructed by new knowledge and the growth of sensitivity. The church must encourage the community, for instance, to change its laws regarding homosexuality. While the church recognizes that the culture has a right to define heterosexual marriage as the norm it does not have the right to define as criminal those who create a different biological and social order. While it is unlikely that homosexuals will ever win the right to be considered normal, it does not follow that the community has the right to persecute them via the law. Insofar as most modern psychiatric knowledge views the homosexual as an emotionally disturbed personality, it cannot simultaneously view him as a criminal personality.

The church honors the right of a civilization to define its norm; but because it views the creativity of a civilization as other than divine, it believes that that norm must be held gently. If a civilization is to be *grandly human* and not merely idolatrous, its standards must be held relatively; such is the double responsibility of a civilization which marries order and freedom.

Our second assumption is that the new morality is no more a final answer than was the rigid morality which it sought to correct. The apparent nihilism of the new morality is little more than a reaction against a system of middle-class ethics which had absolutized its sexual order. The new morality aims at loosening-up Victorian structures, structures which had mixed human creativity with God's creativity. Excessive relativization must be understood as an answer to excessive absolutization. Christianity, committed to man's total humanization, cannot be comfortable with a system which identifies the divine will with a social norm. Christianity is committed to the *dogma* that no man (or woman) is queer before the eyes of God, although he may seem to be so by conventional standards. The redemptive mercies of God are not limited to those who exist within statistical normalcy. The church can be grateful that the new morality has shaken easy absolutes. The church may have followed the line of least resistance and identified itself with bourgeois institutions but the living God is not a shopkeeper.

At the same time the church must be as critical of Bohemianism as it is of the middle class. If the norm of the middle-class man cannot be equated with the divine neither can the exceptions to the norm be made into a quasi-religion. The disciples of a more experimental attitude toward sexuality are not free from metaphysical pretension; chaos is not the goal of human creativity. The goal is achieved as man is enabled to honor process by being flexible, to honor structure by achieving definition. The church must be sympathetic to man as he achieves his definitions and as he holds those definitions with gentleness of spirit.

Our third assumption is that Christianity must be careful of its commitments lest it forget that full sexuality must arise out of true bisexuality. This is to say, the

[106]

answer to the ancient hypocrisy of a double standard, the notion that Joseph is free and the Madonna is bound, is not to equate the Madonna with Joseph. The disinterested observer cannot help but suspect that the new morality is, in part, motivated by a desire to ease sexual tension by eliminating the mystery and individuality which makes bisexuality possible. One of Lady Chatterley's weaknesses was that she, in her pursuit of freedom, took on the sexual patterns of the male. Without suggesting a return to the medieval Madonna, the church, in its defense of bisexuality, must affirm what modern man forgets, that the female expresses her sex with psychological and biological overtones that are radically different from those of the male.

The church, because it is dedicated to full humanity, must resist any system which subordinates or identifies one sex with the other. Victorianism made woman into a passive creature and minimized her right to a sexual being. The new morality emancipated her from that passivity. But the form that this emancipation took was to recreate her as a psychological male. She was given the right to orgasm but in the process the values that she might bring to that orgasm were ignored. The proof of this reductionism is that it is the Victorian female who is considered to be deficient. The male is understood as normal. Yet if there is to be a true mutuality the male must also be transformed; he too must learn from the feminine. Does anyone really imagine that the woman can be healed by reshaping her in the image of one who is enormously mythological about his virility? Is it only the female who needs to be emancipated? If our culture took bisexuality seriously, would it not recognize that the male must also receive from the female a sense for sexual aesthetics? Sexuality without mutual orgasm is meaningless, but at the same time, orgasm without tenderness and responsibility is also meaningless. It may be that the process of maturation will enable us to see that we have undertaken only the first step in emancipation, that we have yet to see the male submit his chaos to a more meaningful purpose.

Fourth, while the church cannot help but underwrite human sexuality it must not make the mistake of identifying humanness with orgasm. Our libidinal culture, struggling against a restrictive view of sex, virtually makes orgasm the keystone on which man builds his humanity. But orgasm is scarcely a human dimension. While the church must include sexuality within the redemptive it cannot accept sex as the center of personality. The new freedom has not really made sex more natural; it has merely made sex more available.

Once man achieves some freedom from the polemical debate over freedom and restriction, he may discover that sexuality in the present stage (including Freudian) of our culture actually impedes communication. The pressures from a libidinal metaphysics certainly have not made possible easy and natural conversations between the sexes.[21] Inasmuch as man is a complicated being he

[21] Recently this writer had the pleasurable experience of a conversation with a very natural nun. The fact that her sexuality had been sublimated made her, Freudianism notwithstanding, a more rather than a less interesting person. In a strange way the

can scarcely be free so long as that element of his personality which he shares with the animal world is made into the center.

It may be that the healthiest thing we can say about sexuality is that we do not yet really understand it. Man is on a journey and he is not yet at the end of it. The thrust and the parry of the contemporary debate may mean only that the two madonnas have not yet been fully synthesized.

Although the church must refuse to identify any of the world's forms with the divine it does provide its own alternative to both the freedom expressed in sexual experimentalism and the continuity expressed in the cultural institution of marriage. But what it offers cannot be transposed into a universal for the world, because its structure for sexuality depends not upon law but upon grace. What it offers to those who are prepared to understand and subordinate themselves to that grace is not an institution but an existential covenant. It offers men and women the possibility of repeating in their relationship the everlasting faithfulness which God disclosed in Jesus Christ.

There is a profound psychological difference between the institution of marriage and an existential covenant. Psychologically the institution of secular marriage suggests a contract which is legally binding. For the secular man the emphasis is on the contract or, to use the vernacular, a knot is tied. The Christian, on the other hand,

---

elimination of sexuality seemed to increase and release her femininity.

does not enter into a contract but into a dynamic relationship under God. The Christian recognizes that the ceremony is merely the introduction to a life under grace. It is that life under grace that makes a marriage; the ceremony merely points to the life which is to come. The ceremony opens the partners to what God is yet to do rather than memorializing a contractual relation.

The existential covenant cannot be dissociated from life within the church. For those who seek merely a legal relationship the church cannot help. That kind of a relationship is a part of the world's "making." The church makes possible a relationship which is continuous and yet fresh, a relationship which is possible because of the treasure of grace. For those who can subordinate themselves to that treasury, there is no suffocating institution.

If the reader assumes that the distinction between an existential covenant and institutional marriage is only double-talk, it may be useful to point out that the problem of the distinction is aggravated by a confusing religio-cultural problem. The clergyman, the servant of the everlasting covenant, is also an officer of the state and its institutionalization of marriage. The uniqueness of the church's understanding cannot be appreciated until the minister ceases to be a kind of spiritual justice of the peace and thus by implication an endorser of the whole complex of legal and sociological structures which the legal institution requires.

The existential covenant of the church is a voluntary covenant. If the covenant were separated from the legal institution of marriage, then psychologically the covenant partners would be freer to participate in the grace which characterizes that covenant. They would be less likely to confuse a living relationship with the institutional law which has its seat not in the church but in the civilization.

The subtle but real distinction between an existential covenant and institutionalized marriage will not be clear until the church withdraws from its partnership with the civil authorities. The state has the right to require a legal contract, but the church offers to those who have faith a profoundly different relationship. The legal service must be separated from the covenantal service so that the covenanting partners will know that they are freely bound in grace and not slavishly bound by cultural law.

The church, then, must support the external culture in its institutions, encourage the culture to be flexible, recognize that the culture is in constant process, and not take too seriously positions that are in midpassage. Meanwhile, for those who share its vision, the church offers a new kind of relationship, one which has its origins in the drama of grace, which was first made manifest on Mount Sinai.

CHAPTER FIVE

The
Metaphysics
of
Pleasure

The art of civilization is a demanding one. To bring that art to its perfection a man must triumph over immaturity and inertia.

To achieve a civilization a man must work very hard. But if he only works hard he will end not as a man in a civilization but as a drone in a beehive.

The civilized man needs play, freedom from work and freedom to enjoy the fruit of his work, as much as he needs the fulfillment that can come only from work.

But the contemporary American lives in a modified Calvinist civilization. Calvinism, especially as it hardened in the generations after Calvin, glorified work and left little room for play. The Protestant heritage produced a world in which industry became an expression of religious faith and a world in which enjoyment was suspect. Hard work produced the need for an annual two-week refuge from work, but it did not teach men how to play.

Ordinarily it is assumed that work is difficult and that play is easy. Nothing could be further from the truth. Everyone is all too familiar with the image of the work-drugged housewife. She surrendered long ago, perhaps with some initial bitterness, to the unending demand of her chores. Now she lives on a treadmill of cooking, cleaning, ironing, getting people ready for school, etc. In order to save her energies she creates routines of work and responsibility. After a few years she cannot deviate from her routines or from her standards of cleanliness and order. She loses whatever sense of play she once had. She no longer enters into games with her children, she does not read to them, nor does she want their play to interfere with her activities. She cannot stand to have her life interrupted, lacking the resources to respond to the chaos that play creates.

This housewife has her counterpart in the compulsive businessman. In order to compete he never allows himself time off, or if he does engage in recreation his mind is still occupied with his work. He comes home overnight with a briefcase or a head full of problems. He has little time for his children, and if his job demands travel he soon becomes an absentee parent. The wife is forced to become father as well as mother. Often such a man comes home too tired to be civilized, and when his burdens are great he cannot even perform his role as an affectionate husband.

[113]

A man who is in the service of the demon work cannot play. At best he can only interrupt his work. If he plays at all he must engage in an activity which leaves his mind passive. A trip to a museum, a concert or an opera is labor and not pleasure; at best it is merely meaningless. The art of conversation, because of its high demands, calls for too much effort. Perhaps he prepares himself for the family chaos (the family, like every community of freedom, is bound to be somewhat chaotic) by increasing his martini consumption. Or he becomes a compulsive golfplayer, since it is always easier to enter into the superficial banter of a foursome than to play with one's difficult children. All children are somewhat difficult if they are not robots. Creative play, in which one taps ever deeper roots of energy and understanding than in one's work, is not easy. It is, rather, the art of the civilized man.

Man is not at liberty to make of himself whatever he wants, for he was created in the image of God. He was made to be like God and not a machine or a beast of burden. We have seen that his work must be creative instead of mere drudgery if he is to fulfill his calling. If he is also to be like God he must be free from his work. Like God he must play.

The play of God in the Bible has two aspects. First there comes a time within the life of God when he ceases his "making." Having brought his work to its conclusion he rested on the seventh day. Machines, until they break down or run out of materials, turn out their plastic ashtrays into infinity. But God is not a machine and his creation is alive. His creation is a world in which man can live, and by which man is at the same time challenged. God rests but not because he is tired. He rests when his "making" has come to an end.

The second aspect of God's play involves his enjoyment. He receives pleasure from what he has made. He not only stops but stands back and *sees*, and what he sees excites him and pleases him. "And God saw everything that he had made, and behold, it was very good." And man, made in the image of God, is also called to play. Man must finish his work, cease, stand back and enjoy. If he does not engage in that kind of play he is not in the image of God but in the image of the machine. Man is called not simply to creativity but to *interrupt* creativity. And the civilization of which he is a part must provide him with the opportunity *not of escaping work but of enjoying the fruits not only of his own work but also that of others*. His enjoyment may consist of the stimulation of books or of music or of sports. So long as he is confronted by the imaginative and disciplined work of a human mind, or a significant challenge to his body, he will be called forth from monotonous drudgery.

Play reminds man that he must be inventive. One cannot enjoy a dull conversation, a trite movie or a football game which lacks surprise. Play reminds man that to the routine of his work he must add the dimension of the unexpected. Through play he learns that life is always new, that to be like God is to dwell in the land not only of discipline but also of surprise.

When man is like God he can cease his work. He can

put the routine away not only physically but also psychologically. The woman who greets her husband at the door is not a lackluster kitchen Cinderella. Her man who comes in that door is not a donkey carrying a heavy briefcase. Both have stopped, have brought their immediate work to a completion. They meet each other with interest, with freshness and even with gaiety. That they do not meet in such manner often, that their meeting is likely to be humdrum or worse only means that man has forgotten that as a child of God he was meant for civilization.

At the moment many communist countries are emphasizing hard work. The Chinese People's Republic is contemptuous of Western and bourgeois standards of play. Regimentation, whether in a strictly Puritan society or in modern Peiping, frowns upon play not only because play interrupts work but because play is the enemy of regimentation. Play causes man to stand aside; and to enjoy this standing aside means that he is not a part of the system. Humor and comedy vividly express the play by which man affirms his freedom from the system.

America has become for the communist the symbol of waste and immoral pleasure. It is interesting to note, however, that American pleasure has made serious inroads into the work-religion of communism. Surprisingly, it was not what we intended to do that "got through," but an aspect of our life that we ourselves had insufficiently appreciated. The political arguments of the Voice of America make little impact on a people who have preserved their sanity by mistrusting all political arguments—whether theirs or ours. It was not our defense of the ballot, but one of the ways in which we *play*, that created a diversion within communist culture. In Yugoslavia, in the Soviet Union and in Czechoslovakia, American jazz has become both a symbol of what America is and a masked protest against the pleasureless discipline of the communist order.

American jazz—and Louis Armstrong is the best ambassador America ever had—provided the regimented man not only with an experience of play but also with a type of music which uniquely emphasizes the importance of freedom within order. Why does jazz introduce the freedom that the communist does not find in the political argument? John Kouwenhoven points out this:

> In jazz that unity of effect is, of course, the result of the very thing each of the players is flouting: namely, the basic 4/4 beat—that simple rhythmic gridiron of identical and infinitely expendable units which holds the performance together. As Louis Armstrong once wrote, you would expect that if every man in a band "had his own way and could play as he wanted, all you would get would be a lot of jumbled-up, crazy noise." But, as he goes on to say, that does not happen, because the players know "by ear and sheer musical instinct" just when to leave the underlying pattern and when to get back on it.[1]

When to get on and when to get off illustrates the relationship between imagination and discipline, between work and play. All music, of course, embodies both structure and inventiveness; but it is jazz which under-

[1] Kouwenhoven, *op. cit.*, pp. 52–53.

lines the *freedom* within music. The regimented man, apparently, discovered in jazz

> the importance of timing, and hence the delight and amusement of the so-called "break," in which the basic 4/4 beat ceases and a soloist goes off on a flight of fancy which nevertheless comes back surprisingly and unerringly to encounter the beat precisely where it would have been if it had kept going.[2]

Again it needs to be pointed out that man is a complicated being. Just as flesh cannot be separated from spirit, time from eternity, so also play and freedom cannot be separated from work and discipline. The hedonist who is interested only in play and pleasure is as far from the Bible as was the Puritan who outlawed pleasure and made a religion out of discipline. The Christian understanding of pleasure cannot be separated from its understanding of work. Man must welcome automation—not because he will be replaced by the machine but in order to gain the freedom to be more inventive. To be creative a man must go off "on a flight of fancy which nevertheless comes back surprisingly and unerringly to encounter the beat precisely where it would have been if he had kept going."

The references to jazz have warned against equating civilization with "highbrow" tastes. Play of many kinds is indispensable to a man, and it would be immature to distinguish arbitrarily between "high" and "low" play. Both forms of play are important for full human exist-

[2] Kouwenhoven, *op. cit.*, p. 56.

ence. It is true that the man who, through no fault of his own, has never had the opportunity to experience the play in a Mozart symphony, has been deprived. It is also true that the self-conscious intellectual (who may enjoy Mozart greatly) is also deprived if he is unable to participate in the banter by which men erase each other's pretensions. A man who imagines that all art belongs in a museum cannot understand the art of a great quarterback like Bart Starr. Both Mozart and the quarterback have the capacity to *astonish* as they suddenly, God knows from where (which is not an exclamation but a theological comment), move beyond the range of technique to some new movement that no one could have anticipated. Both lead the observer along a known path and then, as by an act of God, they introduce him to the new and the unexpected. Man requires in himself—in the play in which he engages—an assurance that at the center of his ordered life there is a spirit of freedom. Only play proves and demonstrates this freedom.

Christianity must fight for the relationship of play and discipline on two fronts. It must be critical of every attempt to create a culture that claims to be "free" because it is uncontrolled. It must simultaneously criticize its own tendency to support a "work" culture. Man was not meant to be either a playboy or a drone. Work divorced from play makes man into a machine. Play divorced from work makes man into a pursuer of pleasure. Both play and work must be bound together so that man can stand back and enjoy civilization he has helped to make.

It is unfortunate that the element of play has been

[119]

minimized in the Christian tradition because, in quite another way, play is central to the Christian life. God has chosen to reveal himself to man in a play. To be sure, the Bible is not a drama in the sense that Albee's *Who's Afraid of Virginia Woolf?* is a play. It is not a work of pure fiction. It concerns a real and historical people, Israel. Yet the history told in the Bible is not well understood unless Scripture is seen as unfolding drama. If the Bible were merely history, if it came to the reader not as a story but as an objective account of certain events, then what it had to say would be unarguable and uninteresting; and it would not be directed toward the greatest center of imaginative play—faith. Does it sound strange to speak of faith as a form of play? Obviously, play is not in this connection to be thought of as playing *at* something. Play, like faith, is an act of the creative imagination. The God who discloses himself in the Bible has so constructed his own Scriptures—his "play"—that man's existential involvement is invited.

Søren Kierkegaard pointed out that God first traps man with a general story before he reveals that man is himself a participant in that story. Kierkegaard illustrates his point by the story of David and Nathan. First Nathan tells a moving tale of a rich man who stole a poor man's only sheep. Then, after David's sense of justice had thrown him on the side of the poor man, Nathan informs him that the story is not as it seems, for "You are the man."

And so it is with each Christian. He reads the Bible and sometimes finds it dull. Reading on, he becomes interested in the story, and suddenly he is shocked to discover that *he* is in that story, that the tale of sin and salvation is not something which happened long ago but that it concerns him acutely. He is taking part in the drama, and finds that he is one (or many) of the characters about whom he has been reading.

God meets man in a play, in the drama of the Bible, because God himself is an artist. This is how he can best address himself to human freedom, speaking as the free God to free men. The religious man who becomes worldly would prefer to get the answer to all his questions about God without the risk involved in believing a story. He would rather have God demonstrate his existence by rational arguments, or he would like to see God prove himself directly by performing miracles. This was the easy, automatic proof that Jesus was asked to furnish. But every time that man pins his hope on gaining the power to make the Bible yield up solid facts with which he can feel secure, he only hears a distant whisper: "This is my beloved son."

The *play* that believing demands, the risk of all that a man hopes for, cannot be found except through the dramatic mist through which God speaks. One cannot wipe the mist away, for it is the assurance of freedom. It is as though God said, "Do not come to me with mere curiosity. Unless you are willing to take the risk of my drama you cannot cross the abyss which separates us. Between me and thee is the mystery and the danger of language." One cannot find God by peering through a microscope or by measuring the stars. God drops no thunderbolts, he merely calls to human beings through pages that may be full or empty.

Man, because he is in the image of God, is the lord of nature. He can build machines to control nature, but he himself was not meant to be mechanical. Like God, his destiny is creativity. Man's sin, as we have seen, consists of his rebellion against fulfilling his complex role. Maintaining a balance between discipline and freedom, work and imagination is, he feels, too demanding. He chooses, on the one hand, to be a beast of burden or a machine, or, on the other, to drift and accomplish nothing.

But he is not content merely to redefine himself. Since all that is in him tells him that he is like God, he is compelled to redefine God if he is to have any peace. He either takes away God's freedom or he takes away his creative discipline. He constructs, alternately, two schemes which will justify himself. In the theological scheme known as Deism he thinks of God as a cosmic engineer or watchmaker who constructs a functioning world and then leaves it alone to work according to the laws that He has built into it. The clock, man and his universe, runs on indefinitely and God has nothing further to do. Man merely observes the mechanical laws of nature. God is in a state of disrelation, of perpetual rest. The system opposite to Deism is found in any form of determinism. In determinism God is never at rest. He is rather the direct cause of all that happens. Generally speaking, Christianity flirts with determinism, whereas the secular or independent mind, if it has any place for

God at all, flirts with a doctrine of Deism which finds God irrelevant to the life of man. But neither determinism nor Deism conforms to the biblical view of God, which sees God as intimately involved in the life of the world and yet free.

It was medieval theology which was especially drawn to the notion of God as power. God was thought of as a great engineer creating and running his factory. He was an all-powerful superintendent not plagued by guilds. What he willed was inescapable. He was an omni-God, all-powerful, all-knowing, always present, always in control. But the omni-God is not biblical; for the Bible respects the withdrawal of God, which we have called his play. On the seventh day God rests. He does not rest because he is tired. He rests because he is not a machine, because he has finished his task and because he desires to stand back and see and enjoy that which he has made. The Sabbath, the Puritans notwithstanding, is the perpetual reminder that man too is not a machine, that he must not only produce but must withdraw from his work, stand back and enjoy.

It is the Sabbath which links man to God. A machine does not need to enjoy, it is fulfilled merely by its incessant productivity. But man, like God, must be free to enjoy the fruits of his work.

Man cannot serve God merely by laboring. The Sabbath demands that he be free, that he derive pleasure from his personal and collective work. Pleasure, the freedom to determine how and what one likes, belongs as truly to the life of faith as service and worship do. He who worships truly but cannot enjoy what man has made fails to understand his destiny as surely as he who denies God and frantically attempts to live by pleasure alone.

Play is the moment of rebirth, that supreme instant when man ceases to be automatic. When he laughs he unconsciously reproduces the Sabbath. One remembers that the machine can do many things that man can do. It can outwork him but it cannot laugh. The machine knows no Sabbath, for only man can play.

CHAPTER SIX

The
Antihuman
Heresy

The hero of Mozart's *Don Giovanni* and God's Messiah have opposite movements. Don Giovanni, almost a symbol of man's pursuit of the ideal, seduces an infinite number of women. He knows that there is safety in numbers; as long as he is moving on he will not be trapped. The pathos of Don Giovanni is that that which he seeks so desperately he can never have. No man ever pursued woman more and no man ever possessed her less. For woman is never a series; she is always one. And so Don Giovanni is lost, not because he seems to possess a prodigious sexual appetite but because he is unable to catch up with an eternally retreating ideal. He cannot become flesh and enter into a concrete relationship with one woman with whom he becomes one flesh.

Like the Flying Dutchman he is doomed to wander forever. His movement is always away from the concrete.

The movement of the Messiah and his church is always the opposite; it is always from the general to the concrete. So Paul says of Jesus and the Christian life: "Have this mind among yourselves, which you have in Christ Jesus, who, though he was in the form of God, did not count equality with God a thing to be grasped, but emptied himself, taking the form of a servant, being born in the likeness of men" (Philippians 2:5–7).

Had Don Giovanni been Jesus he would not have allowed himself to be trapped into being a Jew. He might have worn Jewish clothes for a day or two and then moved on to a new series of carnivals. But Jesus did not move on. He allowed himself to be trapped, for being trapped is the only way one can be human. The movement of Christ and his church, when it is faithful, is always toward the concrete.

The concrete is always civilization, a venture into family, government, education, industry and the arts. Faith can never be expressed abstractly. It demands a homeland in just laws, in graceful architecture, in creative work and in all that makes life pleasurable.

Christianity is a very frail vessel and, like every sinful institution, it is reluctant to risk itself in creativity. How else, for instance, can one explain the chaos and ugliness of some Protestant worship? How else, on the other hand, can one explain the failure of the Catholic tradition (including the Episcopalian) to view the sermon as a creative and prophetic form? Inertia, perhaps the most dangerous form of rebellion, allows each tradition to escape the movement toward the concrete. Protestantism follows Don Giovanni and pursues an infinite number of arbitrary worship services because it does not want to be trapped into a concrete liturgy. Mechanically reacting against the Catholic tradition, it uses freedom as a mask for chaos.

If the Christian movement is toward the concrete and the committed, the heresy which eternally inflicts itself upon Christianity is the Don Giovanni heresy, the separation of the ideal from the particular. And it is this tendency to separate the ideal from the real, God from the world, the soul from the body, which defines what we will call the *antihuman* heresy.

The early church achieved a *formal* victory over this heresy through its Christology. Two movements coalesced to ensure that the church would begin its journey, at least, with a clear understanding that the ideal and the real, the soul and the body, go together. On the one hand, it cast out the Docetists (with their purely spiritual Christ) by insisting that in Jesus the church found nothing less than full humanity. Following the New Testament vision of a bonding of eternity to time (see John 1:14 and Galatians 4:4) the church, at the council of Chalcedon (451) affirmed:

> Following the holy fathers we teach with one voice that the Son (of God) and our Lord Jesus Christ is to be confessed as one and the same (Person), that he is

[127]

> perfect in Godhead and perfect in manhood, very God
> and very man. . . .[1]

In Christ two worlds were merged and, as a result, the human achieved permanence by becoming an accessory of the divine.

The antihuman heresy always attempts to tear apart while the Christian faith always insists upon a union. The ideal is not presented as an abstraction. In Christ, the ideal woman is always one's wife. In Christ, the ideal church is just at the corner. In Christ, the ideal government is that one which the citizen is working to improve.

Although Christianity in its early theology and creeds set itself resolutely against the metaphysics of division, nevertheless, the faith to hold life in union could not always be sustained. Medieval churchmen, following Augustine and heavily influenced by the philosophy of Plato, built a faith which set the soul over against the body, the heavenly city against the earthly city. In the later Middle Ages, Catholicism was able to adjust itself by turning from the dualism of Plato to Aristotle. The great contribution of Aristotle was the insight that the ideal and the real were united, that there was no ideal man apart from real man. Plato's philosophy was that of *division*, and by contrast Aristotle's was that of *fusion*. And the philosophy of fusion, parallel to the Christian doctrine that Christ was truly God and truly man, gave impetus and direction to Catholic civilization. The

[1] Ferm, *Readings in the History of Christian Thought* (New York: Holt, Rinehart and Winston, Inc., 1964), p. 177.

proudest monument of medieval Catholicism, the Gothic cathedral, came into being during the time when the church thought in terms of fusion rather than division. No one who has ever visited the cathedral at Chartres, Thomas J. J. Altizer notwithstanding, can help but be overawed at the merger of faith and stone. The almost incredible beauty of Chartres proclaims the unity of God with his world. The stones seem to intone gracefully that God and man are reconciled.

Here we will not concern ourselves with the ways in which the Catholic Church deals, well or badly, with the implication and the challenge of fusion. What is more important for us to discuss is the way in which Protestantism eludes the full force of its own faith, the conviction that God is no alien Deity, that he, in the incarnation and the atonement, has declared his life to be completely compatible with human destiny. Two major metaphysical heresies that threaten Protestantism arise, first, out of its failure of nerve in regard to a doctrine of the church; and second, out of its somewhat mechanical response to the Bible and especially the thought of Paul.

In part, Protestantism fails to develop a doctrine of the church because of its constant awareness of Rome and its unwillingness to make Rome's mistakes. Because Rome, it seems, has a strong doctrine of the church, therefore Protestantism should have a weak one. Rome tends to associate the institutional church too closely with God, and therefore Protestantism separates the institution of the church entirely from the action and presence of God. The Protestant church becomes an expression of order, but scarcely a house of God. It is content to consider itself a human, all too human instrument where God is worshiped but where he is not uniquely present in the speaking of his Word. Moreover, unwilling to break with the sacramental tradition, it is at the same time unable to exploit the meaning of its own sacramental life. That is why the Eucharist is added as a kind of four-times-a-year afterthought.

In the centuries since the Reformation, the Protestant church has increasingly lost confidence in its authority, and today seems to have almost no self-confidence at all. It has been weakened by its guilt in having made so small or so late a contribution in the battle for racial justice. It has been embarrassed by its own apparent entrapment within the small world of suburbia. Its theologians have ignored if not condemned the church. Even more has it been ignored by the world of literature, having failed to stimulate the birth of novels comparable to those arising out of the Catholic and Jewish traditions. It has been unable to communicate either to its own membership or to the world its magnificent tradition of biblical scholarship, its awareness of God's grace as defined by the Reformation tradition of justification and sovereignty. Uncertain of its own message, it has allowed itself to be represented to the world by a glamorous and peripheral figure, a crusading evangelist. Trapped by its own inner uncertainty it has scarcely realized that such crusades have substituted an emphasis upon morals and will power for the original conviction of grace. The conclusion is almost inescapable; the church has not spoken, it has abdicated.

Having lost or thrown away large parts of its grand legacy, it has, furthermore, been unable to accept itself as an *eccentric* voice. Having nothing left to be different about, it has hungered to be accepted by the world as normal. It is pleased when a distinguished theologian asserts that cultural creativity represents the latent church. It is even happier when a bishop writes a book assuring both the church and the world that the church never meant all the apparently childish things that it had been saying. Those who were not pleased by the evangelist are comforted by a theologian who assures them that they are at least being relevant. Apologetics and strident evangelism both miss the point. Apologetics deflects the eye of the church from its vision and causes it to be caught up in the confusion of the world. Strident evangelism shouts, seduces, threatens, but it cannot celebrate. And, surely, the one deed which the Christian has to give to the whirling world is his celebration of the fusion of God into man's common life.

By fusion we do not mean, obviously, the identification of church and culture. We mean, rather, that the church must witness to the Messiah who has come, to the redemption which is here. God's blessing is fused to man's here and now. God's promise is not a receding hope; it is an assurance that the years of alienation are over, that man lives in the age of the Messiah, the age of benediction, the age when God has bonded his own life to man's future.

The inability to take itself seriously as church means that the church is unwillingly to take *fusion* seriously. All it takes seriously, in a schizophrenic way, is its own dilemma; or else it ignores the dilemma, hoping that its problems will go away. Since it cannot conceive of itself as being the domicile of God, it can only think of itself as human, a body engaging in the worship of something which is beyond and outside itself but not creative *within* itself. But to see God as outside the church is to ignore the fact that it is the *presence* of God which justifies and indeed creates the possibility of celebration. Either the church will become otherworldly and thus depreciate the Incarnation, or it will depreciate the uniqueness of the Christian life by identifying its existance simply with "the good life." In either case the church will have surrendered to the antihuman heresy by denying the message which it has been entrusted to give to the world—namely, that God and his transforming power are present here and now. Yes, the divine risk is present even within the stumbling, uncertain community of faith.

Paul is clearly Protestantism's most conspicuous, if not its only, saint. The central importance of Paul had been neglected in medieval theology. Indeed, as Luther discovered, the medieval emphasis upon work-righteousness had virtually, although perhaps unconsciously, made Pauline thought irrelevant. Thus the dramatic recovery of Paul by Protestantism understandably gave him a singular authority. As long as Protestantism remained Protestant (instead of disintegrating into humanism) it possessed few resources for yoking Paul to that aspect of God's revelation which he had not experienced.

More than any other New Testament writer, Paul laid the groundwork for understanding the work of Christ and God's renewal through grace. Paul gives little comfort to the antihuman heresy. God is no alien; he is to be found within the historic reconciling work of Christ. The age of Christ is not an age still to come; it is upon us in our here and now. Paul does not conceive of a rich eternity and an empty time; he knows only eternity which gives and time which receives. "But when the time had fully come, God sent forth his son, born of woman . . ." (Galatians 4:4).

Paul's sense of the reality and the fulfillment that came in Christ provides the eternal foundation for Christianity's rejection of an abstract religion. The church should not, following Paul, worship a God who somehow, somewhere exists. In a sense the church does not worship God at all. Rather, it is *witness* to His coming. Humanists, Deists and Unitarians may bow their heads reverently before some abstract principle of divine order. Those who have been taught by Paul do not worship in so abstract a way. Rather, the church proclaims the Lord's death till He comes. It witnesses, happily, to a God who is here and now. We do not worship an antiseptic being hidden in some foreign Olympus. God does not remain in heaven. He does not even remain on the mountaintop. He comes down into the valleys, into human existence, and there frail and ungodlike (from the point of view of the heretics) he is seen by human

[133]

eyes. The earthly manifestation of God, the fulfillment within human conditions, provides, as Paul well knew, a problem for all those who can believe only in an abstract God.

> Where is the wise man? Where is the scribe? Where is the debater of this age? Has not God made foolish the wisdom of the world? For since in the wisdom of God, the world did not know God through wisdom, it pleased God through the folly of what we preach to save those who believe. For Jews demand signs and Greeks seek wisdom, but we preach Christ crucified, a stumbling block to Jews and folly to Gentiles, but to those who are called, both Jews and Greeks, Christ the power of God and the wisdom of God. For the foolishness of God is wiser than men, and the weakness of God is stronger than men. For consider your call, brethren; not many of you were wise according to worldly standards, not many were powerful, not many were of noble birth; but God chose what is foolish in the world to shame the wise, God chose what is weak in the world to shame the strong, God chose what is low and despised in the world, even things that are not, to bring to nothing things that are, so that no human being might boast in the presence of God. He is the source of your life in Christ Jesus . . . (1 Corinthians 1:20–30).

Paul's somewhat satirical contrast between wisdom and foolishness illuminates the difference between the heretics who are too sophisticated to recognize that God could be seen and heard in the "ugliness" of the flesh and the innocence of the foolish who, having known God in the flesh of Jesus, recognize that flesh is grandeur and not garbage. He cannot, following Paul, seek God

[134]

above. Rather, one finds him among men and, like men, in the flesh. Paul both magnifies Christ and glorifies that human condition, that concrete life which is so difficult for the metaphysicians to understand.

Paul lays the foundation for a valid Christian humanism. "If God is for us, who will be against us?" Humanism in the ordinary sense of the word reacts against the Pauline doctrine of Christ. Curiously, this ordinary humanism finds it difficult to believe that God is other than distant and abstract. Equally curiously, Christianity, which is often accused of being antihumanistic, holds the highest possible view of man in that it witnesses to the "holiest" manifesting itself in the "lowest." That lowly humanity in the Pauline Christology becomes precious indeed.

Paul had not personally witnessed the total revelation of the Word made flesh. He knew the glorified Lord; he did not know, in the same way that the authors of the Gospel traditions did, the earthly and prerisen Lord. And Christian theology, following the total witness of the Bible, must be bound by the historical Jesus as well as by the risen Lord; they are one and the same.

Without the Jesus who walked the roads of Palestine, who called his disciples, who healed and who wept, who was led as a criminal to his death, the church does not have the whole Christ. The Gospels give us the Christ of lowliness and humiliation; Paul gives us his humiliated Christ as the Christ of glory. Together they make possible a faith of fusion, in which the Word truly was made flesh.

[135]

There have been misdirected followers of the Gospels who ignored the risen Lord and saw Jesus merely as a teacher of ethics. There have also been exclusive followers of Paul who saw Jesus only as a risen, wholly spiritual Lord; or to be more precise, who saw the risen Lord as wholly spritualized. Such "followers" of Paul (who deplored any personal following attached to himself) ignore some of Paul's own teachings about the lowliness of Christ.

> And being found in human form he humbled himself and became obedient unto death, even death on a cross. Therefore God has highly exalted him and bestowed on him the name which is above every name, that at the name of Jesus every knee should bow, in heaven and on earth and under the earth, and every tongue confess that Jesus Christ is Lord, to the glory of God the Father (Philippians 2:5–11).

When the humanity of Jesus is forgotten, the gospel turns sour, and the spiritual Lord is used to attack the flesh. Hatred and contempt for man constitute the first sign of such an incomplete understanding of God's revelation. The notion that man is worthless or evil represents the most serious distortion of the New Testament. Those who separate the risen Lord from his earthly life hopefully may discover that despising man is not the same as honoring Christ. It is always easier to hold man in contempt than to see him redeemed by Christ. *Within faith there is no possibility of pessimism, just as within heresy there is no escape from it.*

[136]

If the believer is to escape the antihuman, the metaphysical heresy, he must be sure that he binds Gospel and Epistle together. One cannot build a theology exclusively on Paul's response to the risen Lord. Thus if one tried to understand Christ solely from the following passage one would not have the whole Christ: "From now on, therefore, we regard no one from a human point of view; even though we once regarded Christ from a human point of view, we regard him thus no longer. Therefore, if any one is in Christ, he is a new creation, the old has passed away, behold, the new has come" (2 Corinthians 5:16–17).

Paul, limited by the fact that he had known only the risen Lord and not the Jesus who had walked the streets of Jerusalem, places too little stress on the flesh of Christ, and as a result Paul tolerates too radical a separation between old and new, between flesh and spirit, between creation and redemption.

If one reads with Paul the Sermon on the Mount (Matthew 5–7) then one understands not that the new has eliminated the old but that God, in the mystery of Christ, has bound Good Friday and Easter, flesh and spirit, old and new together.

Just as there is an Old and a New Testament, so too is there the fleshly Jesus of the Gospels and the glorified Lord of the Epistles. Just as faintheartedness often sets the New Testament against the Old (by raising it above the Old), so too the temptation arises eternally to divide the Christ. When one reads how Paul spoke to the Gentiles, and forgets, his Hebraic background, then often the heresy of the Gentiles, spirituality, obliterates the Hebraic paradox of spirit and flesh bound together.

It was the Greek-speaking philosophers of Paul's day who, largely because of the influence of Plato, were deterred from the theology of fusion. Whereas the Jews had accepted life in the flesh as a gift of God, many of the philosophers had seen the flesh as at best a frail and shoddy imitation of eternity. Paul, speaking to Greeks, may have been too much influenced by their aversion to a unity of flesh and spirit. It was in Athens that Paul was first mocked for his doctrine of the Resurrection. Furthermore, the Greek minimization of flesh had a point. Unlike Hebrew culture, the Gentile world had not been able to maintain a creative balance between flesh and spirit. The emphasis upon spirit was itself a reaction against a gross misuse of the flesh. Over and over again Paul is shocked by the moral degeneration of the pagan culture that he faced (see Romans 1:26–27). Paul, as he faced Gentile culture, was forced to choose between the higher moral discipline of those who were at least leaning toward "spiritualism" and those who had morally distintegrated in the port towns of the Mediterranean world.

It must be kept in mind that Paul faced a special situation. *The necessity to spiritualize the gospel disappears when one faces a creative instead of a degenerate civilization.* One comes to a different evaluation of the flesh within the painting of a Breughel, the sound of a Mozart, and the flesh of a fulfilling marriage from that within the context of a brothel culture like Corinth's. Flesh is

[138]

just as much flesh in a statue of Michelangelo as it is in a pornographic picture. Flesh is just as much flesh in Verdi's *Aida* as it is in a lewd song. Flesh is flesh, but the form in which it is presented changes the challenge of flesh. And Paul, facing the moral decay of the ancient world, cannot be blamed for counteracting the disintegration of the flesh with what might appear to be an overemphasis on spirit. At the same time, those who live in a world where flesh is not only beautiful but also bears the signs of the divine imprimatur—as it does in marriage and art—know that one must follow Paul in his positive doctrine of the flesh and not in his corrective arguments against a decadent civilization.

God, as Paul saw, came into the world; and that world, as the whole Bible testifies, came under the jurisdiction of the kingdom. God came into the world not that the world would be destroyed but that it would become his dwelling place. God came into the world not that man might go somewhere else but that man might make the world just and true and beautiful.

It takes disciplined faith to yoke Paul with the Gospels. The faith that he communicated was given not that man would become the prisoner of Paul but that he, in conjunction with the whole witness of the New Testament, would have the courage and the creativity to see what Paul saw, and say it truly for a world whose destiny is to become the kingdom of God.

CHAPTER SEVEN

The Gift
of
Hope

The church cannot truly be the church if it either isolates itself from or identifies itself with civilization. It must support man's "making" so long as it is creative, suggest corrections when that "making" becomes chaotic. It can do this, as we have seen, by contributing *hope* to human creativity, toward justice, toward the end of racism, etc.

But it must do more than contribute. Indeed, it cannot contribute at all unless it also has an inner life, a piety in which its total attention, hearing and worship is turned toward Him whom it daily celebrates. It can give hope only insofar as it dares to possess a center apart. It can be related only insofar as it dares to be disrelated, for only inasmuch as it has a private life can it also have a public life.

The task of contributing to the world's hope while living inwardly is a double one. If the church does not recover its inner life it will merely absorb the world's despair and its illusions. If it does not support the world's "making" with its gift of hope it will become merely a vault for musty doctrines. If it did not receive from God, the church could not contribute to the world. If it failed to speak out of its legacy and be informed by what is happening in the world, the church would become, as it often has, fossilized.

The church must understand the world, for what happens within the world often happens within the church. Even when the church retreats from the world it often absorbs dimensions of the world that it has rejected. There is a curious parallel between science and theology in the seventeenth and twentieth centuries. The seventeenth century, whether theological or scientific, thought in terms of tight systems. Newton (1642–1727) created a cosmology based upon fixed and exact laws. In the same period Protestant Scholasticism froze the fluidity of the earlier Reformation and gave an equally fixed form to revelation. The Helvetic Consensus Formula of 1675 pressed its conception of orderliness to the point where it could argue that even the Hebrew vowel points had been inspired by God. This conclusion can only have been the result of a tidy rationalism, since the vowel points were added centuries after the canon was closed.

The twentieth century, on the other hand, has seen

both theology and science break loose from their seventeenth-century moorings. The "new physics" and the "new mathematics" have broken with regimented structures, and twentieth-century theology is equally fluid. Whether or not there will be abiding merits to Bonhoeffer's "religionless Christianity" or to the death-of-God theology, they are related to the greater freedom created by Vatican II and the imaginative reconstruction of a church theology by Karl Barth.[1] The age of largely doctrinal thinking is past, as both science and theology testify to a spirit which resists reducing either God or the universe to a formula.

The church must be bound and yet free. Unlike the death-of-God theologians the church must recognize that it is controlled and defined by its inheritance (whether God lives or not is surely more than a matter of language). Unlike the theological conservatives the church must recognize that much of its language actually violated its legacy. And, as this book has been suggesting, the church must recognize that secularism often moved into a vacuum created by the church's lack of courage.

Perhaps the greatest disservice that the church did to its legacy was to organize much of its thought around

[1] The achievement of a more imaginative apparatus has not been seen without resistance. There seems to be an unholy alliance between some Catholic, some Protestant and some secular thinkers. Father Gommar A. De Pauw's Catholic Traditionalist movement, and the crypto-Calvinism of *Christianity Today* each attempts to make a monument of a fluid legacy. Many social scientists operate with the kind of fixed empirical standards which are closer in spirit to the rigidities of Newtonian physics than to what is happening in the physical sciences.

[142]

the distinction between *the natural* and *the supernatural*. The intent of this refracted Platonic concept was to protect the holiness of God, but the effect was a divorce between God and the world. Indeed, the language of natural and supernatural denies, if we can believe St. Athanasius, the intent of the Nicene Creed. In his treatise on *The Incarnation of the Word of God* he says that "the renewal of creation has been the work of the self-same Word that made it at the beginning. For it will appear not inconsonant for the Father to have wrought its salvation in Him by Whose means He made it."[2]

The uniqueness of Christianity has been not the separation of God and man but their "union" in such a way that their true individualities are protected. The ancient legacy conceived of God and man in terms of dramatic intimacy and reciprocity. As Irenaeus saw it the Incarnation bound two worlds together "so that God should forever teach, and man should forever learn."[3] The jettisoning of the artificial concept of the natural and the supernatural not only allows the church to move back into a world which it had erroneously vacated but as its reward makes possible the recovery of intimacy which characterized the biblical understanding of God and man.

[2] *Nicene and Ante-Nicene Fathers*, Second Series, ed. by Schaff and Wace (Oxford and London: Christian Literature Publishing Company, 1892), vol. IV, p. 36.

[3] Irenaeus, *Against Heresies*, Book II, Chap. 28, par. 3. In *The Ante-Nicene Fathers*, vol. I, ed. by Roberts and Donaldson (Buffalo, N.Y.: The Christian Literature Publishing Company, 1885).

The Christian knows nothing of an alien God. His celebration is of One who is both Creator and Redeemer, of a Messiah who in ascending into heaven brings man permanently to the throne of God.

If one thinks in terms of the unity of the divine and the human which God initiated and made permanent, he will not be confused by the heresy of thinking that there was an impassable gulf between God and man. By using a split terminology, the church tempts the world to adopt the false position of glorifying what it believes to be the natural, leaving the church concerned only with the spiritual, the transcendental, and the supernatural. The Christian must witness to one world, because God has committed his presence and power permanently to the human situation. The world may be unbalanced in its judgment of man but the church dare not be. To the church has been entrusted the task of understanding the fullness of man. To do that it must cultivate the poise— and poise is always the posture that faith assumes as it resists frenzy—to accept the "corrections" from the world and shape them to fit a more mature view.

The world needs salvation, not erasure. Salvation purifies human existence: it does not eliminate it. The world may seek a universe without God, but the church dare not seek a God without the universe. All that is precious in the legacy bids the Christian to hold fast to that world which a good God shaped and into which He breathed the breath of life. All that humanity dares hope for is sustained by Him who became flesh.

Naturalism, itself the defensive child of a bifurcated

view of reality, is as subject to idolatry as the church is to otherworldliness. It makes little difference whether one makes a human system into God or whether one escapes the human venture by fleeing into a fleshless eternity. The emptiness of Christian "spiritualism" is matched by the idolatry, as we have seen, of an empiricist culture which makes a single tool into the total answer to meaning. Both leave men passive and lifeless. And it is surely the task of the church to move from bifurcation and grasp the unity at the basis of reality.

Even sin cannot be used to separate man from God because insofar as sin involves the moral rather than the metaphysical it does not affect man's ultimate nature. Furthermore, since Christianity is a witness not to the sin but to the victory of Him who overcame it it is meaningless to think in terms of an abyss between God's world and man's. Or as Irenaeus put it: ". . . He passed through every stage of life, restoring to all communion with God."[4] And so man possesses a higher stature than either naturalism or supernaturalism can imagine.

The Incarnation of the Logos forever ends all dualism, even that ancient dualism between flesh and spirit. "The flesh, therefore, is not destitute [of participation] in the constructive wisdom and power of God."[5] Man's body as well as his soul becomes sacred. In the flesh he is also spirit. In the body he is yet in the image of God. Amid the dirt and the slime a light shines and there is no longer slime or dirt. Man, every man, belongs to the

[4] *Ibid.*, Book III, Chap. 18, par. 7, p. 448.
[5] *Ibid.*, Book V, Chap. 3, par. 3, p. 529.

[145]

light and therefore the church can only look at him with hope.

Today the world is fatigued with its own despair. In redesigning man as only natural and merely mortal it made him not into a child of glory but into a high-class animal. Man is not an animal, and he is as much demeaned by comparing him to the animal world as he was earlier etherealized by comparing him to beings in a supernatural world. Today the church must take the initiative. The day of its retreat is past. It must now affirm to a waiting world that the world stands and that man abides because God has thrust Himself permanently into the human condition.

Civilization must be corrected and redirected when it loses its courage and its hope. But the church can only correct the world by first correcting itself. Christian otherworldliness failed not only because it arose out of fear of the world, a fear that God did not share, but because that otherworldliness was itself a deviation from the biblical faith. Partly, the church failed because it could not quite believe that the news was good, that what God had wrought in the Resurrection was a reconstitution of man himself. A faith made nervous by the cynicism of the world could not quite take God seriously. The church suffered its failure of nerve even though the voice of the Bible was clear. So far as the Bible is concerned, it has no knowledge of a life for man apart from the world which God created for him. God not only made that world and saw it to be good, but He remained faithful to the world even while the world lost faith in itself. God not only did not destroy that world but sent His Son to replace drift and world-weariness with purpose. Furthermore, when the world attempted to escape life by destroying the Son, the false empire of death was destroyed by the Resurrection. The biblical faith, so extraordinary and so glorious that the church itself cannot quite bring itself to believe it, affirms the permanence of that reconstituted world.

> Then I saw a new heaven and a new earth; for the first heaven and the first earth had passed away, and the sea was no more. And I saw the Holy City, new Jerusalem, coming down out of heaven from God, prepared as a bride adorned for her husband; and I heard a great voice from the throne saying, "Behold, the dwelling of God is with men. He will dwell with them, and they shall be his people, and God himself will be with them; he will wipe away every tear from their eyes, and death shall be no more, neither shall there be mourning nor crying nor pain any more, for the former things have passed away" (Revelation 21:1–4).

The kingdom of God is not only a new heaven but also a new *earth*. God does not destroy earth: matter, flesh and existence abide. The fulfillment of what God made comes as a purification and not as a destruction of His original creation. The kingdom is new only in that the old has been turned back to where it was before it had been detoured into death and sin. The kingdom of God comes to mankind, and His presence assures against any harm that might befall man. The believer is assured that nothing will be different except that "death shall be no more, neither shall there be mourning nor crying nor pain any more, for the former things have passed away." Out of such a faith the church must speak to a world still hypnotized by the cobra of death. The world waits for the foolishness which is wiser than its own sophistication. It waits, consciously or unconsciously, to hear some one sing, "yea" to life. God willing, the singer will be the church.

A nature-oriented world has declared that it is not interested in an ethereal and postnatural existence. In doing so, even with distortions, the naturalists have honored the world that God created. The naturalists and even the pagans have reintroduced phases of the divine activity which the church had spurned. It would be sinful of the church to continue to be charmed with a fairy world when modern man has discovered God's real world. That modern man seems to be unaware that the goodness of that real world has something to do with its Author, and that the love and aspirations of a Godless world are always distorted, is not the ultimate issue.

To accept the real world demands that the church regain its nerve. To recover nerve requires that the church become again a laughingstock. The only climate in which the church can truly be itself is the climate of the paradoxical. For it is the grasping of two positions in radical tension which the heart requires. The easy answers of the church are the answers of either relevancy or irrelevancy. A theology of relevancy merely says what the world says and adds lamely that God is somehow mixed up in the process. A theology of irrelevancy is

[148]

one in which the church retreats from the human hope as it spins a tale of an eternal life and isolates it from the real world.

To affirm that God's victory is here and now is to meet the world at the point where its perceptions have failed. God's victory—His bonding of His purpose and His power to human fragility—means that, in fact, man is strengthened and shaped for endurance. Whether or not one believes it, God is at work overcoming through human knowledge and techniques the enemies of life.

In a world where He is present, one may expect the continual lengthening of life expectancy, just as one may be confident that an increase in political sophistication and morality will reduce and finally eliminate the occasion for war.

But the world cannot believe the good news that the bonding has taken place and, unable to believe, it deceives itself with its so-called realism. It has purchased not life but death. For man cannot have zest for life if he is *resigned to death*. But the human heart weeps: for, although it fears the void, it yearns for life. Man, true man, is not a passive, accepting being. He is a challenger and a creator. He is built for life.

Modern culture is built around a death cult. A vigorous but uncritical naturalism has joined forces with existentialism and Freudianism in asserting that maturity requires man to bow to an inexorable mortality. The death cult is in part merely a reaction against the facile assertions of eternal life expressed by Christianity. Never-

[149]

theless, Christianity is now put in the position, as it thinks of man's permanency, of seeming to engage in nothing more than wishful thinking, whereas the naturalists credit themselves with realism.

But a death orientation is no more natural than a life orientation. In the center of his consciousness, man is incapable of assuming the end of consciousness. Consciousness cannot imagine its extinction. Man, to be sure, draws conclusions by observing the possibility if not the certainty of the grave. He may even succeed in cowing consciousness: but he can do no more than that, for from the point of view of consciousness, all observations about death are only hearsay. At the same time, the church has no more evidence that death has been overcome, as man observes it, than the so-called naturalist has the power to eliminate from consciousness the suspicion that death is unnatural. The contest between what consciousness knows and what observation deduces ends in a draw.

But the gift of its hope is possible only if the church chooses to be unashamed of the drama in which it is involved. To the world which has come to the point of trusting only the provable, the church can merely say: "We offer you not proof but a story." And the story that is offered is a living, unfinished story. Its characters are still being cast. Auditions are very trying. The world may well decide that it would like to know the outcome, to have some guarantees before it risks its life and independence in a play whose success is not guaranteed. But there are no guarantees! Only machines can function without risk or insecurity. But neither the gospel nor the human heart can be mechanized. Without risk no truth can be won. God, one speculates, might have arranged an easier victory for men and for Himself. Perhaps He could have arranged it so that His truth could be determined by a test as simple as one contained in a schoolboy's chemistry set. Perhaps to secure even more assurance God's truth could have been warranted by having it tested and vindicated by a committee of the world's foremost scholars and scientists.

Perhaps! But a mechanical test could not engage the imagination. God's truth reaches man's poetic not his engineering sense. The truth can be discovered only when it becomes personal, and as each individual is committed not to simple facts but to venture. There is no safe way to know God. There is only the way of personal commitment, of danger, for those who hope to be *human*.

But if the church is to overcome its own timidity it must tell its story honestly. No fumbling. No evasions. No double-tongued lines. The direction must be clear and the characters must be true. Those who are called to speak their lines must be caught up in their rhythm, and not intrude either fear or boasting. Shakespeare's counsel must apply to the church: "Speak the speech, I pray you, as I pronounced it to you, trippingly on the tongue: but if you mouth it, as many of our players do, I had as lief the town-crier spoke my lines" (*Hamlet*, III, ii, 1).

The lines must be authentic. The play only requires actors who have both the meekness and the audacity to tell the story that the Bible tells, that God has glorified

[151]

the world and made it permanent. The church must not mouth its lines in embarrassment, and then in relief join the world as it makes a religion out of death.

A young novelist, John Updike, has caught the players as they avoided the paradox and mouthed their lines. In a poem called "Seven Stanzas at Easter" he says:

> Make no mistake: if He rose at all
> it was as His body;
> if the cells' dissolution did not reverse, the molecules
>   reknit, the amino acids rekindle,
> the Church will fall.
>
> It was not as the flowers,
> each soft Spring recurrent;
> it was not as His Spirit in the mouths and fuddled
>   eyes of the eleven apostles;
> it was as His flesh: ours.
>
> The same hinged thumbs and toes,
> the same valved heart
> that—pierced—died, withered, paused, and then
>   regathered out of enduring Might
> new strength to enclose.
>
> Let us not mock God with metaphor,
> analogy, sidestepping, transcendence;
> making of the event, a parable, a sign painted in the
>   faded credulity of earlier ages:
> let us walk through the door.

That stage must be walked on boldly, for both the human heart and God are concerned with *His flesh: ours.*

⁶ From John Updike, *Telephone Poles and Other Poems* (New York: Alfred A. Knopf, Inc., 1963), pp. 72–73.

The church will not be victimized by the world's unwillingness to risk the absurd or even what is merely implausible. What is believed must be told: not only that, in Christ, death has been overcome, but that the man whom God made has become eternal. The Athenians laughed at Paul and the world will laugh at faith because those who are afraid to hope would rather accept death mechanically than risk what faith promises— eternal life. Every funeral procession will prove man's absurdity. Every death will point the contradiction between what is believed and what seems to happen. And faith may die if, crumbling in face of the contradiction, it rewrites a more plausible drama. But faith comes into its own only at the point where the contradiction is accepted, where the lines spoken are grasped by an ultimate trust. For man made *in the image of God,* can settle for nothing less than life, true life and life in the flesh.

God is truly long suffering. He continues to work through that motley band of players who cannot quite accept the lines He has so graciously offered. While He takes upon Himself the suffering of the world in order that the world might be healed, His church allows its eyes to wander. God looks with joy and confidence upon the world that He made and which He has guaranteed while His players, embarrassed by the divine miracle, direct their attention elsewhere. The church, weak in faith, cannot bear the contradiction. It would rather be irrelevant or trite than absurd. But God is not put off. The story remains. It only wants for actors who will believe

[153]

their lines and who will not be tempted to ad lib when the world begins to laugh.

All that God has told of Himself tells faith that His movement is toward man and not toward some alien world. "Thy kingdom come. Thy will be done, on earth as it is in heaven." Humanity is locked into God's world by Him who "was crucified, dead, and buried; He descended into hell; the third day he rose again from the dead: He ascended into heaven, and sitteth on the right hand of God the Father Almighty; from thence he shall come to judge the quick and the dead."

Grace locks the believer into the lines that he must speak. Renewal is inescapable. Escape is unnecessary. To accept is to love the world. Humanity can cope with the beer can on the highway: it is only temporary. Man need not, and the church dare not, make a cult out of death. Man is neither a machine nor a beast nor a corpse. For him God has assured lordship and eternal life. Alive and aware that death has no dominion, he rises above fear and lethargy and inertia. The nerve of courage is restored. He becomes open and curious. He struggles. He raises questions. He becomes troublesome, for such is the character of those who are lords and not robots. He lives as a troubadour and he sings "yea" to life.

The play comes to an end. But just before the final curtain the modest voice of the Good Shepherd whispers, "Surely, I am coming soon." Those who are busy rattling their programs and putting on their coats do not hear that voice. For them the magic is over as they go out into the darkness which they cannot escape. They

[154]

can only whimper, "And how am I to face the odds of man's bedevilment and God's? I, a stranger and afraid, in a world I never made." Those, however, who have not only heard the voice but have believed, reply, "Amen, come Lord Jesus!" For them there is no darkness at all.